_____ Along the Arun _____

John Adamson

John Adamson
November 2014

The Alexius Press

First published 1994
Second impression 2000
Revised edition 2014

Published by
The Alexius Press
114 Sandhurst Road
London
NW9 9LN

ISBN: 978-0-9519886-8-8

A CIP catalogue record for this book is available from
the British Library.

Typeset by Barry Redhead with Richard Dukes

Design and colour reproduction by
Aylesbury Studios Ltd, Bromley, Kent

Printed and bound by CPI Group (UK) Ltd.
Croydon CR0 4YY

CONTENTS

LIST OF PHOTOGRAPHS

Photographs were taken by Vlasta Smith (VJS),
Derrick Sillience (DJS) *and Barry Redhead* (GBR)

LIST OF MAPS

Key

— — — Recommended route   ✛ Church or chapel

PREFACE

Since the original version of this book was published in 1994, much has changed in one part of the area covered by it – there has been a major redevelopment along the east bank of the Arun at Littlehampton. Elsewhere, particularly in villages and the countryside, there has been less change, but nevertheless a full revision of the book has been necessary to take account of the effects of the passage of time, and on a practical level modifications of the recommended route have proved desirable. There is much to be seen, of course, away from the route, and this edition of the book gives greater indication of alternative paths. The Ordnance Survey Map 121 - Arundel and Pulborough – provides a valuable source of reference.

While some energetic readers of the book will wish to regard it as a guide to a long-distance walk and follow substantial sections in a single outing, many people - particularly those with cars – may well prefer to explore only comparatively short sections of the route at one time. *Along the Arun* can, indeed, be used as a straightforward guide book by readers who are disinclined, or are physically unable, to follow footpaths which are not always hospitable places particularly in wet weather. I hope that the book will also appeal to armchair travellers with a bent for local history.

When I wrote the first edition of this book I felt that the part of England it covered was of exceptional interest and beauty and on my numerous visits while working on this new edition I have been confirmed in that view. Places cannot, and should not, remain frozen in time and where changes have been necessary - as at Littlehampton - these have, in general, been well considered and positive in their effect.

In revising this book I have been greatly assisted by librarians and archivists who have provided guidance on sources and also in some instances given me the benefit of their personal knowledge and experience. I would like in particular to acknowledge the help given at the West Sussex Record Office, Chichester and Worthing Libraries, the Sussex Archaeological Society Library, the British Library and the London Library. Local knowledge was specially important to give an understanding of the changes at Littlehampton. The Arun District Council gave useful leads and I should like to express my appreciation of the help given by Juliet Thomas, Curator of the Littlehampton Museum; Billy Johnson, Littlehampton Harbourmaster; Geoff Warminger, associated with the lifeboat; and local residents who provided useful insights informally. Acknowledgement is made to Faber and Faber, publishers of Philip Larkin's *The Complete Poems*, and to the poet's estate, for permission to use the extract from *An Arundel Tomb* which appears on page 49. The typesetting and design skills of Barry Redhead, who was assisted by Richard Dukes, made an important contribution to the development of this book. Jeremy Adamson gave valuable help on IT aspects.

I hope that readers derive as much pleasure from exploring the Arun Valley as I have done.

John Adamson
August 2014

INTRODUCTION

Natural features of the landscape such as rivers and hills are not just the background to people's lives today, but form a link with the innumerable generations which have preceded us, and beyond them with periods of time whose distance is difficult for the mind to grasp, over which the Earth took its present form. It is, for example, superficially strange that the River Arun, like its Sussex neighbours the Adur, the Ouse and the Cuckmere, arises not in the high ground of the South Downs, but in the comparatively flat land of the Weald.

To understand how that situation has arisen we need to go back to a time between 110 and 65 million years ago when Sussex and, at times, most of England, was under the sea. During that time chalk, which consists mainly of crystals secreted by planktonic algae, was deposited. Earth movements then lifted the chalk into the shape of a dome over what is now the Weald, with what became the North and South Downs forming a rim. The Arun and its neighbours rose on that dome, and gained there the momentum which enabled them to cut their way through the Downland valleys where they now run. The chalk which formed the centre of the dome was then eroded, leaving the rivers to pursue their placid courses with only a modest fall between their headwaters and the sea

It is now thought that some 20,000 years ago the Arun, like its neighbouring rivers, ran south of the present coastline to join a Channel River flowing west, which was also fed by rivers flowing from what is now France.

The discovery of the shin bone of an early human at Boxgrove near Chichester was until recently thought to be evidence of the first known Briton, who lived some 500,000 years ago. The Boxgrove site provided evidence of what we might now call the lifestyle of those who lived in the area, for along with the bones of large animals were found the tools used to butcher them. There is, however, no line of descent from the humans of that time to ourselves, as the branch of humanity to which Boxgrove Man belonged is believed to have died out.

The early history of humans in Britain was largely determined by the relation of Britain to Continental Europe – at times connected, at times isolated – and by the advance and retreat of ice during the Ice Ages. The mild conditions which meant that the Boxgrove people had abundant animals to eat came to an end some 450,000 years ago, when ice advanced almost to the current line of the Thames, with conditions south of that equivalent to those which now exist near the Arctic ice cap. Evidence for the subsequent sequence of events is far from complete and sometimes open to more than one interpretation but points to a long absence of any part of the extended human family until about 60,000 years ago when traces have been found of Neanderthals. Under circumstances which can only be a matter of speculation the Neanderthals were supplanted by Homo Sapiens, modern man, and we can envisage our earliest direct ancestors as appearing as groups of hunter-gatherers some 25,000 years ago, then moving to and from Britain as geological and climate changes permitted. These groups came to form larger and more settled communities as hunter-gathering gave way to agriculture. It remains unclear how far these developments in Britain derived from new waves of people and how far from changes in the way of life of the indigenous population.

We can identify that by 3,000 BC the transition to farming was well advanced. The increasing organization and sophistication of society was demonstrated by the building of such a structure as Stonehenge. Sussex has nothing as dramatic as Stonehenge from this period, but what are known as causewayed camps – areas surrounded by banks and ditches which are broken by ditches – are to be found, one at Bignor Hill on the South Downs close to the Arun Valley.

Subsequent developments can be traced by changes in burial practices and by the adoption of bronze and then of iron. Hill forts survive from the Iron Age (including The Trundle, near West Dean, north of Chichester) and the archaeological evidence is joined by written, as we recognize the Celtic peoples described by Julius Caesar in his *Gallic Wars*.

The Belgae, an Iron Age people who arrived about 75 BC, may well have founded a city on the coastal plain in the Selsey area. No trace remains of that, but within the area covered by this book evidence of the Belgae survives in the Arundel area, as mentioned in Chapter 6. It is the Belgae who provide us with the first recorded name of a political leader who held sway over what we now call Sussex – Commius, King of the Atrebates, a tribe whose area of control stretched along the South Coast between the present-day towns of Eastbourne and Bournemouth, and ran north as far as the Berkshire Downs. Commius had previously been King of the Atrebates in Gaul, and was sent to Britain by Julius Caesar as a preliminary to his inconclusive invasions, which took place in 55 and 54 BC. Commius returned to Gaul with Caesar in the latter year, but then changed sides, joining the revolt of the Gauls under Vercingetorix, escaping back to Britain when the revolt failed.

Following the death of Commius the Kingdom of the Atrebates broke up, and when the next - and decisive - Roman invasion took place in 43 AD, under the general Aulus Plautius who had been sent by the Emperor Claudius, there was something of a re-run of the political situation which obtained at the time of Caesar's invasion. As on that occasion the Romans, while facing some hostile tribes, could rely on a degree of British support. In the Claudian invasion, the rôle previously adopted by Commius of the Atrebates was taken by Togidubnus of the Regnenses, the name given to that part of the Atrebates who were centred on what is now Sussex.

Togidubnus had his reward in being established by the *Romans* as what the British in India would have called a "Native Prince". He remained loyal to Rome during the revolt of the Iceni under Boudicca, and his status and the regard in which he was held by the Romans is illustrated by the Palace at Fishbourne which was almost certainly his headquarters during the latter part of his reign. It was possibly during the reign of Togidubnus that the Regnenses established their capital at the site of what is now Chichester. In Roman times that city was known as Noviomagus, a Celtic name meaning "new city on the plain", illustrating the fact that although it was typically Roman in its plan and its features such as Amphitheatre, Forum and Basilica, it was not a directly and exclusively Roman foundation. The name Chichester, which sounds of Roman origin, comes in fact from a Saxon root, possibly deriving from Cissa the son of Aelle the invader of Sussex mentioned below - although it has been suggested that the writer of the Anglo-Saxon Chronicle to whom we owe Cissa's name may, in fact, have invented the person to explain the place name.

Stane Street, the Roman road from Chichester to London, crosses the route of the walk in this book, and near the route is the large Roman villa at Bignor which has fine mosaic pavements. While this villa would have been the centre of a substantial estate, like those subsequently constituting manors, much of the countryside remained in the possession of individual farmers continuing broadly the pattern of life they would have had before the Romans arrived.

The collapse of Roman authority in the early fifth century A.D. left the Romano-British inhabitants of Sussex, as of the rest of Britain, struggling to maintain their society in the face of political uncertainty and military threat. The written and archaeological evidence of subsequent events in Sussex is sketchy. The Saxons under their leader Aelle may have settled initially under treaty, or as conquerors from the beginning; the date of their arrival (thought to have been on the Selsey peninsula) is given by the *Anglo-Saxon Chronicle* as 477; although recent scholarship has suggested a date twenty years earlier than that. The subsequent Saxon conquest lacked the speed and decisiveness of the Roman which preceded it and the Norman which followed; according to the chronology of the *Anglo-Saxon Chronicle*, it took the Saxons fourteen years to reach and take the fort of Pevensey.

There has been much scholarly debate about the extent to which there was a continuity of development between Romano-British and Anglo-Saxon society. The evidence is not, and never can be, conclusive. Those who feel the strong sense of continuity with the past evident even in modern Sussex, and can appreciate the great isolation of individual families and communities which must have been a feature of a Sussex whose landscape included much forest and swamp, are likely to suspect that however great the political upheavals which historians now strive to understand, the life of many of the common people will have continued on lines which had been set for many generations.

The Saxons have left their mark in the Arun Valley in the form of the fortified site at Burpham, described in Chapter 8. A Saxon origin is also claimed for Arundel Castle although no trace of Saxon work remains. The Saxons' defences were built against Viking/Danish raiders; in due course it was raiders such as these who had settled in France and achieved comparative respectability as Normans who were to conquer England.

The South Saxons briefly re-established as a political unit the territory which had been occupied by the Regnenses, but following a battle in 607 they became tributary to the West Saxon kingdom, and never regained full independence during the often confusing shifts of power which marked the centuries before the Norman Conquest. Sussex did not, however, by any means drift into isolation from national politics. Godwin, who is thought to have been the son of the Sussex thane Wulfnoth, was Earl of Wessex and one of the most powerful men in the kingdom during the latter part of the reign of Cnut (1016-35), the reigns of Cnut's sons Harold (1035-40) and Harthacnut (1040-42), and the early part of that of Edward the Confessor (1042-66); Edward married his daughter Edith in 1045. Six years later he fell from favour; his career curiously prefiguring those of some of the Earls of Arundel and Dukes of Norfolk described later in this book, except that Godwin was sufficiently strong, and disloyal, to force the King to restore him to his position of power.

Godwin's son Harold achieved such a position as political figure and military leader that he became King after the death of Edward the Confessor. In accordance with Edward's wish and with the support of the leading figures in the country he succeeded to the throne in spite of not being in the royal line of succession. It was from Bosham, one of the Sussex manors which he had inherited from his father, and from which Godwin had gone into exile in 1051, that Harold had set sail on the expedition to Normandy during which he is claimed to have sworn loyalty to Duke William - a sequence of events recounted in the Bayeux Tapestry. Whatever the precise significance of these preliminaries to the Norman Conquest, the outcome is, of course, well known - the invasion of England by William, and his victory at Hastings, in 1066.

An important thread of continuity between the Saxons and Normans was provided by the Christian Church. In 681 - 84 years after St. Augustine of Canterbury had started his mission in Kent - St. Wilfred and a band of followers had landed on the Selsey peninsula and initiated the conversion of the South Saxons. They were given land at Selsey which became the seat of the South Saxon bishopric. In 1076 the seat was moved to Chichester but the boundaries of the bishopric remained the same. In ecclesiastical architecture, it is often difficult to distinguish Saxon from early Norman work.

After the Conquest, Sussex was divided by William the Conqueror among his nobles; Arundel was the base for Roger de Montgomery's share of the county. Chapter 4, in following the history of the Earls of Arundel, gives some indication of the subsequent political events which would have impacted on the people of Sussex, although much normal life must have continued uninterrupted by the conflicts mentioned. More serious disruption was almost certainly caused by the French invasion of 1216 in support of barons in revolt against King John; it was not until the next year, after the King's death, that the invaders were driven out.

Troubles with the French recurred during the second half of the fourteenth century when raiding was frequent, and in Chapter 9 there is reference to that time in relation to the fortification of Amberley Castle. The naval exploits of Richard twelfth Earl of Arundel mentioned in Chapter 1 were in reaction - albeit rather belated - to the threat of raids and perhaps invasion.

Amid the uncertainties of medieval life stood the Church, the pervasive influence of which was evident not only in the parish churches and diocesan organisation but in monastic institutions, in which Sussex was particularly rich - some feature in this book. For a time these institutions must have seemed part of the natural order of things, set to endure for many centuries.

The reality proved very different. In the 1340s, Sussex, like the rest of England, was struck by the plague known as the Black Death. Its effects - compounded by those of the French raids mentioned above - were devastating in many aspects of the county's life, social, economic and religious. Up to a half of the county's population is thought to have died as a result of the Black Death's most virulent impact, in 1348 - 49; monastic institutions were struck like other sectors of the population. Many villages were deserted and it may well have been as a result of the Black Death that Ilsham, the site of which is described in Chapter 3, became a "lost village".

The combined effects of plague, war, poverty and oppression led to the Peasants' Revolt of 1381. There was an impact in Sussex even though it was not one of those counties mainly affected. Although in the next century Sussex was again involved in an irruption of popular anger - Jack Cade's rebellion of 1450, which was motivated by a mixture of political and economic grievances - in general the fifteenth century in Sussex saw economic improvement and the consolidation of civil society, helped by the county's comparative immunity from the upheavals of the Wars of the Roses; and in secular society progress was maintained in the sixteenth century.

The story was very different in the religious sphere. The idealism of the monastic movement had waned with the passage of time, and within that movement- as indeed within the Church as a whole - a spirit of service had tended to be replaced by remoteness, laxity of observance, and pursuit of wealth. When, during the reign of Henry VIII, Cardinal Wolsey and then Thomas Cromwell set out to close monastic institutions and appropriate their property, therefore, they were able in many parts of England, including Sussex, to do so without, in general, a great deal of public protest.

Later in this book references are to be found to a number of monastic institutions which fell victim at the time of the Reformation. While views on the usefulness of the monastic way of life vary, many people will feel in contemplating the ruins of monastic houses some sense of loss at a tradition destroyed; also, in an age which has seen many upheavals of its own, some sympathy with the monks, friars and nuns rudely uprooted from their (usually) cloistered existence. Happily, many were redeployed, as we should say nowadays, into parish work; others received pensions.

Continued religious tensions are reflected in the story of the Dukes of Norfolk as set out in Chapter 4, and in divisions within Sussex society which affected the attitude people took at the time of the Civil War. In that conflict Sussex was not the site of any major battles, but there were a number of clashes of arms in the area - those at Arundel being described in Chapter 6. Although there was some settling of Civil War scores after the restoration of Charles II, in general a comparatively gentlemanly attitude was adopted throughout a turbulent period during which districts, classes and families were divided in their loyalties.

The eighteenth century was something of a golden age for aristocratic Sussex families, whose wealth and taste were demonstrated in building and landscaping, and whose influence was exercised through artistic patronage and political activity. In the latter part of the century, the fashion for sea bathing led to the development of seaside resorts - Chapter 1 refers to this process in relation to Littlehampton.

Beneath this calm surface, however, there was much turbulence. Agricultural depression and enclosure led to impoverishment, and a major source of employment in the county was smuggling. While this activity has acquired a certain romantic aura, the reality was much grimmer, with smugglers employing intimidation backed by murder to enforce acquiescence in their activities, and a number of pitched battles being fought between smugglers and the forces of law and order.

In the early nineteenth century, pressure caused by overpopulation and poverty, and exacerbated by the effects of a system which placed responsibility for relief of the poor on the individual parish, led to discontent which culminated in the "Captain Swing" rioting of 1830. The Poor Law Amendment Act of 1834, by grouping parishes for the relief of poverty, and greater economic activity related particularly to development in transport, led to improved conditions, and Sussex settled into a less turbulent era.

Up to the eighteenth century Sussex had been notorious for the poor condition of its roads, crossing the Weald being very hazardous in winter. Later in that century there was a great improvement in Sussex roads because of the building of turnpikes, run by Turnpike Trusts which were authorised to levy tolls on road users. Nevertheless, in an era when road travel was by horse-drawn coach, the benefits of road improvements for the personal traveller (there were also benefits for the farmers) were very much concentrated on the well-off; in no way did a system of mass transport exist, and facilities for movement of large amounts of freight remained very inadequate.

The nineteenth century saw a remarkable improvement in what we should now call the transport infrastructure. Earlier measures to facilitate the navigation of rivers were supplemented - the action taken in respect of the lower Arun is described in this book. Canals were built, in Sussex notably the Wey and Arun, which naturally increased trade on both rivers, but also one linking the Arun with Portsmouth, the junction of which with the Arun is on the route in Chapter 3. Far more significant, of course, was the creation of the railway network, which had a profound effect in terms of economic development, and also in terms of the impact on individuals and local communities in providing greatly increased personal mobility. The chalk pits at Amberley, described in Chapter 9, are an example of an industry which benefited successively from canal and railway development.

Inevitably, improved communications, notably in terms of transport but also of large circulation newspapers, radio and in due course television, had the effects of reducing the isolation and distinctiveness of Sussex, as of other parts of England. To attempt to describe the social and political development of Sussex over the last, say, 150 years would, to a large extent, be to record the local impact of national trends and events. Nevertheless, Sussex has retained much of its own character, particularly in areas such as the Arun Valley, which have not been heavily affected by that spread of often ill-planned urban developments which was one of the less happy features of the county in the twentieth century. To maintain this character without stopping necessary change and development is a major challenge. In meeting it a balanced understanding of the past must be an asset.

In the chapters which follow, the threads of the early history of the Arun valley area will be linked with more recent events and with the contemporary scene in a personal interpretation of this beautiful and historically rich part of England. No such interpretation can ever hope to be definitive; both the current scene and perspective on the past are subject to constant change. It is hoped, however, that this account will be found both informative and enjoyable.

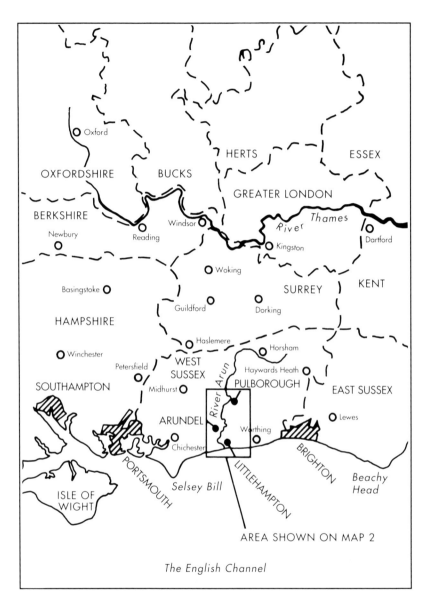

Southern England, showing location of the Arun valley.
Scale 1:1,188,000 - 18.75 miles to one inch.

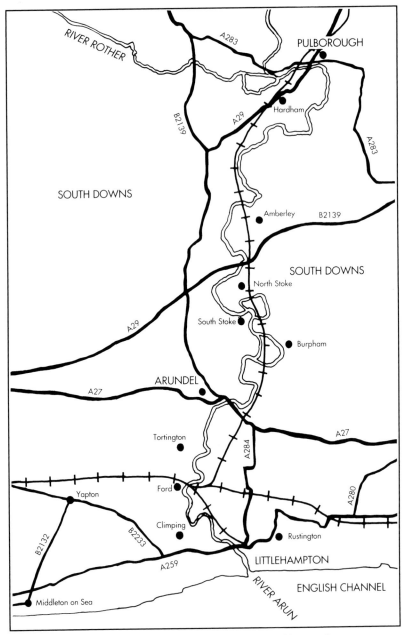

The Arun valley - Littlehampton to Pulborough.
Scale 1:158,400 - 2.5 miles to one inch.

14

CHAPTER 1.

History of Littlehampton

L ittlehampton has the holiday attractions of modern Sussex: beach, amusement park, yachts on the river, open country for walkers. Unlike some other South Coast resorts, however, Littlehampton is not simply the product of the relatively recent desire of the English to take their holidays by the sea. It was originally a port and existed as such in Saxon times under the name Hamtun; the "Little" was a medieval addition, possibly to distinguish the town from Southampton. After the Norman Conquest it was active in the import of stone from quarries in Caen and as the English landfall of great figures of the day. William Rufus landed in Littlehampton in 1097 after campaigning in France and Matilda, daughter of Henry I, is thought to have arrived here in 1139 on her way to Arundel during her campaign to assert her right to the English throne against Stephen. It was also prominent later in the Middle Ages. Richard Fitzalan, the eleventh Lord of Arundel and a major military and naval figure, brought to Littlehampton prisoners taken at the Battle of Crécy in 1346. In 1387 his son, also Richard, who as mentioned in Chapter 4 was Admiral of England, defeated a fleet of Flemings, Frenchmen and Spaniards off Margate, capturing many ships, and went on to capture more on a raiding expedition to Sluis; some of these ships were brought to Littlehampton.

At that time the Arun was not set in its present course, and its mouth was some way to the east of its present position. It has been argued indeed that it was at one time as far to the east as Worthing, but the evidence for this falls short of the conclusive. We can, however, envisage medieval Littlehampton as being not directly on the sea but on a tidal estuary which was separated from the sea by a shingle bank. So far as can be understood, the tendency of the river mouth to be pushed east by the drift of the shingle in that direction was counteracted by the river's propensity to break through the shingle bank to the sea where erosion permitted.

There are records of a number of steps from about 1600 onwards to establish a straight channel to assist navigation. The current channel was established under the Harbour Act of 1733 and protected as it reached the sea by piers on either side. Further action proved necessary to maintain the harbour and regulate the way in which it was run.

Littlehampton Waterfront - the Harbour Office is behind the post

The steps taken were effective in maintaining Littlehampton's position as a port. In the nineteenth century formidable families of ship builders, repairers and owners, the Isemongers, Harveys and Robinsons, dominated the commercial life of the town; the paintings and other exhibits in the Littlehampton Museum convey the flavour of that era. As the glories of the age of sail faded in the face of competition from steam, however, Littlehampton's family shipping firms faded also, although the G. and J. Robinson Company continued into the 1920s.

The middle of the nineteenth century saw a marked increase in activity in Littlehampton harbour as a result of the opening in 1863 of the town's railway station and, as a consequence of that, of the establishment of ferry services to the Continent. These services only lasted some twenty years, however, as they were unable to survive competition from those based at other south coast ports, especially Newhaven. While the harbour continued in substantial use particularly for the handling of agricultural products, timber and coal, a decline set in, which was only briefly arrested during the First World War when it was used for loading war materials required in France.

The town - originally village - centre of Littlehampton was at some distance from both the sea and the river. The course previously taken by the Arun, as already indicated, explains why the village was not built by the sea. The tendency of the Arun to flood was no doubt a main factor in determining that the village should be some way to the east of the line of the river. In medieval times - and indeed as late as the second half of the seventeenth century - the village appears to have consisted only of a church, manor house and a small number of houses grouped round a triangular area which probably served as market place and village green. As indicated in the following chapter, the plan of this original core may still be seen in contemporary Littlehampton.

By the beginning of the eighteenth century the town was expanding to the west, but remaining to the north of the line of what is now the New Road until the Arun's new channel was cut following the 1733 Act. We can envisage the working life of Littlehampton at that time as based partly on agriculture and partly on the harbour.

The second half of the eighteenth century saw the development of a new role for Littlehampton which has continued until the present time - that of seaside resort. The attractions of sea bathing were identified in 1750 in Richard Russell's *A Dissertation concerning the use of Sea-water in the Diseases of the Glands*, and visiting the seaside became fashionable first at Brighton and then at other towns. In the eighteenth century as now, refreshments and accommodation were needed for the visitors. A pioneer in providing these was Peter Le Cocq, a London coffee house owner, who ran the Beach Hotel. As with the other seaside resorts, the end of the eighteenth century and the early part of the nineteenth saw a flurry of building to cater for those who wished to own or rent fashionable properties. This process started in the 1790s at the north-east of the Green, at Norfolk Place, and extended west along South Terrace, although progress became stately in pace – St. Augustine's Road was not reached until the 1870s. The phasing of the Terrace can be detected in the changing architectural style. Beach Town, as this area was called, was separated from the rest of Littlehampton not only by open space but also by some social distance.

South Terrace

The opening of Littlehampton Station in 1863, already mentioned in connection with the development of the harbour, and the improvement of the railway service following the establishment of the loop line at Ford in 1887, which ended the need for shunting between Littlehampton and the main line, were major factors in the expansion of the tourist trade and of the town itself in the latter part of the nineteenth century. The harbour, the old town centre, and Beach Town merged into a single built-up area.

The first half of the twentieth century saw - with the obvious exception of the two World Wars - a growth in tourism. The character of Litlehampton as a tourist resort was changed - to the dismay of some - with the establishment by Billy Butlin early in the 1930s of an Amusement Park, as mentioned in the next chapter.

By the latter part of the 1950s, however, as postwar austerity gave way to affluence, foreign holidays became increasingly popular. By 1958 two million people were travelling abroad, a figure which had increased to three and a half million by 1960 and continued to climb. This had a major effect on Littlehampton and on other seaside towns which relied partly or mainly on the tourist trade.

A striking example of this and other social changes, some earlier and some subsequent, is the reduction in the number of hotels in the town and, more recently, in the number of public houses also.

The Arun District Council has attempted to adapt the town to changing social and economic conditions and some aspects of the effects of its policies are brought out in the following chapter.

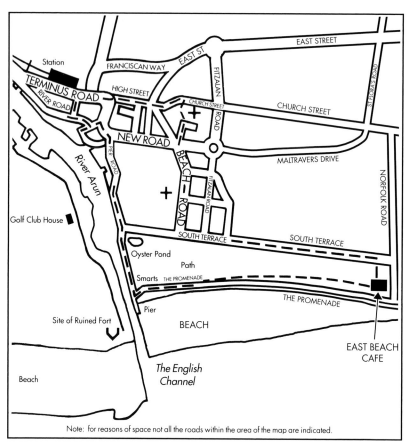

Town map of Littlehampton. Scale 1:15,600 - 4 inches to one mile.

The following labels appear on the map:

EAST STREET
Station
FRANCISCAN WAY
EAST ST
TERMINUS ROAD
HIGH STREET
RIVER ROAD
FITZALAN
CHURCH STREET
CHURCH STREET
ST HORA'S ROAD
NEW ROAD
PIER ROAD
BEACH ROAD
FITZALAN ROAD
MALTRAVERS DRIVE
River Arun
NORFOLK ROAD
Golf Club House
SOUTH TERRACE
SOUTH TERRACE
Oyster Pond
Path
Smarts THE PROMENADE
THE PROMENADE
Pier
EAST BEACH CAFE
Site of Ruined Fort
BEACH
Beach
The English Channel

Note: for reasons of space not all the roads within the area of the map are indicated.

CHAPTER 2.

Walk around Littlehampton

Distance: About a mile and a half.
Walking Conditions: Mostly roads; some firm paths.
Station: Littlehampton.

Littlehampton Station is a convenient starting point for an exploration of the town. From the forecourt the route crosses the main road (Terminus Road) to Terminus Place opposite – although a detour to take advantage of the nearby traffic lights may be advisable. It then runs down Terminus Place and continues straight ahead across a junction into the road signed as Mariners Quay. The pavement to the right of that road leads via a short footpath to the banks of the Arun. The riverside walk is followed to the left up to the point where there is a sign on the embankment wall saying Arun CAAC Riverside Walk Conservation Design Award 2005. The route then turns left past three metal bollards into a road with the signs Netley Court to the left and Wight Court to the right, leading into Surrey Street.

Much of Surrey Street now has modern, Georgian-style residential buildings, and while these have been successful in retaining some of the original character of the area, it is difficult to envisage the lively activity which would have been seen in the late nineteenth and early twentieth centuries, when there were two hotels on the east side of the Street, the Norfolk Hotel at the south end and the Dolphin Hotel at the north, by the High Street. Reminders of the old Surrey Street are to be found on the east side of the Street at No.59 (Old Quay House) and at No.61, formerly the Cairo Club and more recently a restaurant. Surrey Street continues past No.61 towards the river and on the other side of the road is Look and Sea, a complex which has a Heritage Exhibition, Visitor Centre, Riverside Café and Restaurant, and Viewing Tower.

The route follows the river towards the sea, passing the Lifeboat Station and Harbour Office. Where it joins the road - Pier Road - there may be a sign saying Ferry. The ferry concerned, which has run from the end of March to the end of September, has provided access to the West Beach without the need for a detour via the footbridge, to which reference is made in the next chapter. The future of this service depends, however, on the availability of funding. At the end of Pier Road - originally known as Mussel Row – is a pond known as the Oyster Pond because it was once used for storing oysters.

Beyond the pond there used to stand a windmill, the subject of John Constable's painting, "Littlehampton", which was a feature of the Littlehampton scene from 1831 to 1932 when it was demolished by Butlins to make way for an Amusement Park. The site remains in use for that purpose at the time of writing, under different management. The route continues along the embankment. At the south west corner of the Park may be seen the site – now faced by an embankment covered with shrubs – of a fort built in 1759 during the Seven Years' War, at a time when a French invasion seemed imminent. The threat of such invasion was only dispelled by Hawke's decisive victory over the French fleet at Quiberon Bay in November of that year. This fort saw further service as part of England's defences during the Napoleonic wars, but fell into obsolescence and decay during the course of the nineteenth century. A particular difficulty was restriction of the field of fire by buildings to the rear of the battery. The fort was replaced by the one on the west bank of the Arun which is mentioned in the following chapter.

The route follows the bank of the river past the lighthouse to the end of the short pier, from where there are fine views, including one of the line of the South Downs. It then returns past the coastguard station. A tarmac path across the Green, the beginning of which is marked by anchors partly buried in the sand, may now be taken, but the recommended route extends to the east along the promenade to the East Beach Cafe. This was designed by Thomas Heatherwick who was subsequently responsible for the cauldron at the London Olympics and the new Routemaster-style London bus. His declared objective was a building which would fit in with what he described as the raw beauty of the Littlehampton seaside. It has certainly helped to put Littlehampton on the map as a fashionable destination.

The East Beach Cafe

From the East Beach Cafe the route runs across the Green to South Terrace, reference to which has been made in the previous chapter, and then to Beach Road. This is followed, passing the modest but pleasing Marine Gardens and the St. Catherine's Roman Catholic Church, a Victorian building mainly of Kentish ragstone, a form of limestone which is difficult to work and gives a rough-hewn appearance. Past the Church is Caffyn's Field, an open grassed area which has happily been preserved from development. Beyond that, at a road junction, is the well-maintained War Memorial.

Across the junction to the right is the Civic Centre, headquarters of the Arun District Council. The route follows Church Approach by the side of the Civic Centre to St. Mary's Church. It is possible that there was a Saxon Church on this site, but the first Church here of which we have firm knowledge was a medieval building with a squat tower rising from about half-way up the roof. A complete rebuilding took place in 1826 and the Church was again rebuilt in 1934. The path through the churchyard is followed into Church Street, where the route continues to the left. On the right is the Friends Meeting House, originally an infants school built at her own expense by a Mrs Welch, who purchased the site in 1835. Her school was known as a "Penny-a-week" one, after the amount which the pupils were expected to pay to contribute to the costs.

Church Street, Littlehampton

On the left is the Manor House built in the 1830s by a prosperous local farmer on the site of an earlier building mentioned in the previous chapter. It belonged subsequently to Dr John Candy, who founded the local Board of Health. It was then given to Littlehampton Urban District Council in 1934 and became the home of the Museum in 1991. The Museum started in the Library and moved to premises in River Road before establishing itself at the Manor House. It

Friends Meeting House

has interesting paintings, maps and artefacts illustrative of various aspects of Littlehampton's past.

The route continues along the north side of Church Street where there are some pleasing cottages. Nos. 7 (Hampton Cottage) and 9 (St. Mary's Cottage) were once a single house, thought to have been the earliest building in the group. The date of No. 1 (Vine Cottage) is shown as 1727.

After a short while the route reaches East Street at a junction marked by a supermarket. East Street is followed to the left and the route shortly reaches the pedestrianised High Street where it turns right. Like so many High Streets this has lost much of its original character although some interesting buildings remain. The route continues past the Clock Tower to Terminus Road and the Station. The walk may be continued following the directions which begin in the next chapter, although it should be noted that the route of the Littlehampton to Arundel section is the longest in the book, albeit that there is the possibility of making a break at Ford Station.

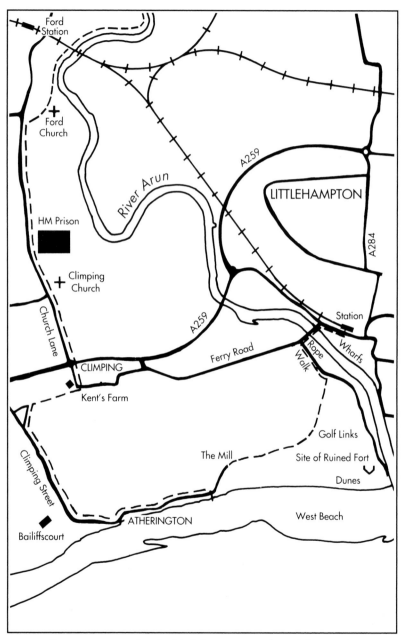

Route map, section 1: Littlehampton to Arundel, part A.
Scale 1:25,000 - 2.5 inches to one mile.

26

CHAPTER 3.

Littlehampton to Arundel

Distance: About seven miles.
Walking Conditions: Paths, mostly firm, and roads, busy ones
                           having footways.
Station: Littlehampton, Ford, Arundel.

The walk begins at Littlehampton Station, from where the route turns right and then crosses the (often busy) Terminus Road/ Bridge Road towards the Arun View Inn, then goes over the Arun footbridge. The bridge is at the site of two earlier solutions to the problem of crossing the river. The first of these was the chain ferry, installed in 1825. This was, in effect, a piece of roadway laid on top of a boat which was pulled across the river by a chain controlled by hand-operated machinery. It was subject to some modernisation around 1870, and replaced by a swing bridge built alongside, which was opened in 1908. This had a fixed span on the west side and, on the town side, a moveable one to permit the passage of shipping. In due course fewer and fewer ships went up to Arundel, and when in 1938 the Ford railway bridge (which previously had a moveable span) was fixed, ships could no longer go beyond there. The swing bridge was replaced by the present footbridge in 1981, road traffic now being catered for by a new bridge to the north.

From the footbridge the route turns left, opposite a sign saying Littlehampton Marina, along a road which is the beginning of Rope Walk, where, as the name suggests, rope was once made. On the left are various buildings, mainly industrial but including the Littlehampton Yacht Club.

It is possible to continue down Rope Walk to West Beach and then walk along the edge of the beach to the west, but walking along the sand and shingle is not easy and the recommended route turns to the right following the Public Footpath sign just before the West Beach Car Park sign. A Beware Golf Course sign is then encountered – the footpath runs to the right.

Trees meet for a while overhead and there are glimpses of the golf course on the left, followed by marshy ground and then the golf course again. The path has become more open, and then after a stretch where the trees once again join overhead the path divides, with Public Footpath signs pointing to right and left. The recommended route runs to the left, towards the sea.

Through the trees on the right can be seen a complex of buildings on the site, and including elements, of Climping Mill. A reference to the Mill has been traced back to the fourteenth century. The mill of which part survives was built in 1799 but it ceased to be used at the end of the nineteenth century and the top storey was removed in 1962.

South of Climping Mill once stood St. Giles Church. This served the parish of Cudlow, of which the path which the route is following was once the northern boundary. Incursions of the sea separated the parish into East and West Cudlow and led to the decline and eventual disappearance of the Church, the last record of which is on a Naval map of 1698.

The path reaches the edge of the beach and is followed to a car park, with café, at Atherington, the name of which has survived on Ordnance Survey maps although unlike Cudlow, and Ilsham to which there is reference later, it was a manor and not a parish. Beyond the car park the road - Climping Street - is followed to the north, care being needed, especially initially, because there is no established footpath. On the left, after a short distance, is the remarkable phenomenon of Bailiffscourt.

Bailiffscourt owes its origin and name to a monastic foundation by the Abbey of Séez in Normandy; the monk who lived at the grange at this site was known as the bailiff of Atherington. Only the chapel, a late thirteenth century building, dates from that time. The manor house in fifteenth century style was built in 1935, along with two adjacent buildings in early medieval style. The other buildings in the grounds, apart from the chapel, and the pigeon house, which is

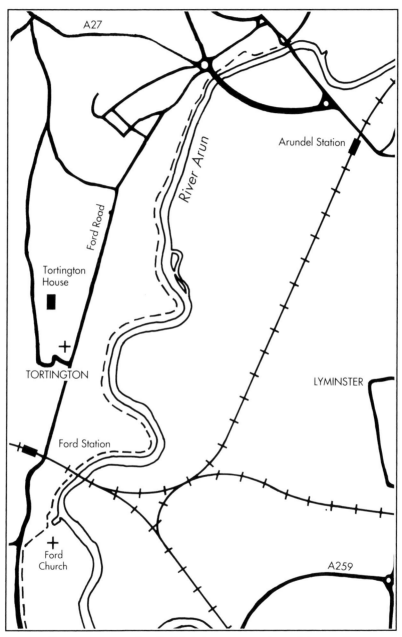

Route map, section 2: Littlehampton to Arundel, part B.
Scale 1:25,000 - 2.5 inches to one mile.

probably eighteenth century, have been imported to form a sort of open-air museum.

The house was built for Lord Moyne who, when minister resident in the Middle East, was assassinated in November 1944 by members of the Zionist extremist organization, Lehi, usually known as the Stern Gang. The assassination was part of a cycle of violence resulting from conflicting claims to what was known as Palestine which continues to this day. Lord Moyne's involvement with this problem dated from his appointment as Colonial Secretary in 1941. This post came after a distinguished record of public service. As Walter Guinness (he was a member of the brewing family) he became an MP in 1907 and was Minister of Agriculture in 1925. He was raised to the peerage in 1932 and thereafter was an inveterate traveller. The peace of the Sussex countryside provides a poignant contrast with the turbulence in distant lands which resulted in Lord Moyne's death.

Bailiffscourt is now a hotel of rather an exclusive nature. Following the road north, one soon reaches, on the right, the Black Horse, an attractive public house which is in the village of Climping. The first certain reference to this pub was in 1843.

A short distance beyond the Black Horse there is a Public Footpath sign pointing to the right but that path may not be usable. The recommended route continues north along Climping Lane past the entrance to Rigates Home Farm on the right. At the end of the subsequent fence there is a Public Footpath sign to the right which indicates a tarmac path, and this is followed. The path veers to the right through fields towards a wind turbine.

At St. Mary's Church of England School an opportunity arises for the walker to return to Littlehampton by following a path which leads to the right and runs through fields before reaching the beach just to the east of Atherington. From that point the beach can be followed right back to Littlehampton, or the route described earlier in this chapter can be walked in reverse.

The route of the walk set out in the remainder of this chapter, however, goes past the school to a junction – Amberley Court is on the left. The route continues to the right until Kent's Farm is reached

Bailiffscourt - Manor House

Bailiffscourt - Chapel

31

on the south side of the road. Based on the core of a late seventeenth century building, Kent's Farm was extended and partly rebuilt in the two subsequent centuries.

Just beyond Kent's Farm is a Private Road sign. Close to this spot was the site of a forgotten Church - probably demolished in the fifteenth century - which served the "lost village" of Ilsham, through the location of which the route has run since passing the School. In the seventeenth century the "Private Road" was known as Ilsham Street but since then all trace of the name Ilsham has disappeared from the area, and the very location of the village had been lost in historical memory until the exemplary scholarship of Dr.T.P. Hudson, set out in his section on Climping in Volume Five of the Sussex volume of the Victoria History of the Counties of England, brought it back to public knowledge.

From a little further along the main road there can be seen on the right, across a field, Brookpits Manor, a substantial, probably mid-seventeenth century, building which may have been at the eastern edge of Ilsham. The route returns along the main road to the junction by Amberley Court and continues to the right along that road to the busy A259. The path is followed to the right until crossing is practicable, just beyond the railing, using a traffic island. The route then runs to the left for a short while before turning to the right up Church Lane at the crossroads. A new housing estate is to be seen across a field to the left and the route passes Church Farm on the right. Soon Climping Church, one of the finest Sussex churches, is reached.

The tower, the oldest part of the Church, had the capacity of providing a place of defence to the villages, as well as a spiritual beacon. The doorway is a fine example of Norman dog-tooth work. Unhappily, the needs of security mean that, as with so many churches, the building is normally closed, so that the fine early thirteenth century interior can no longer be appreciated. Near the tower is the tomb of Lord Moyne, decorated with curious winged animals, improbable denizens of an English churchyard.

There is a road opposite the Church with the signs Rudford Industrial Estate and Café. The café, a modest establishment, is right at the end of the estate. The route continues to the north past Ford Open Prison.

Climping Church: Norman doorway

On the left, on a plinth, is the fuselage of a Hawker Hunter with the marking Royal Navy WW654. This is a very prominent reminder of Ford Airfield, established in 1918 as a training establishment and briefly used by the United States for the training of a heavy bomber force which was to have been based in France but which had not become operational by the end of the war. It remained with the RAF until in the 1930s it came into civilian use mainly for "joy riding" flights. Later in the decade it reverted to the armed services, first under the Air Ministry and then the Admiralty, when it was commissioned as HMS Peregrine and housed the Royal Navy's Air Observers' School. It reverted to the RAF in October 1940 primarily as a base for night fighters and went on to provide a centre for developing operational techniques for the use of radar equipment by such fighters. The Royal Navy took it over again between late 1945 and early 1959. The main part of the airfield was incorporated into the Prison but some civilian flying continued until

Ford - The Ship and Anchor

1971.Some of the airfield buildings became part of the Industrial Estate already mentioned.

Continuing north, a line of poplars on the left is reached, and opposite, across a large field, Ford Church - partly obscured by trees – and, to its left, the Ship and Anchor public house come into view. The route continues to the right along a small road leading up to the Church, but walkers may prefer to continue to Ford Station and resume the route at a later opportunity.

Where the route reaches the fence and hedge at the edge of the churchyard a path is taken to the left. The path turns, following a hedge to the right, then turns again, this time left, along the edge of a field.

At the corner of the field the path runs straight ahead. On the right are boats on what is now a small inlet of the Arun, which is a remnant of the Portsmouth and Arundel Canal. This canal, in association with the Wey and Arun, provided a through route from London to

The Arun at Ford

Portsmouth when it was opened in 1823. However, the canals were uncompetitive in relation to the coastal route and, later, the railways; the Portsmouth and Arundel was a viable proposition for less than twenty years, although it was not officially abandoned until 1896.

The route continues onto the Arun embankment and turns left along it, soon running under a railway bridge. Arundel Castle may now be seen to the left but the Arun winds to the right. To the east, across not only the river but the railway line, the tower of Lyminster Church can be seen. This tower was built around 1200 but the existence of the Church can be traced back to about 880.

The river next sweeps left through a rather featureless landscape. In due course, as the river turns once again, the village of Tortington comes into view across the Ford Road. The first prominent building to be seen is the seventeenth century Manor Farm built in red brick.

Behind that is the Church of St. Mary Magdalene. North of these buildings is the substantial Tortington House built close to the end of the seventeenth century. After a number of changes of family ownership it came into educational use in the twentieth century, first as a Catholic girls' boarding school and then as the English campus of New England College at Henniker, New Hampshire.

Past Tortington the river swings once again to the right, with Arundel appearing ever more clearly on the left. At the next bend in the river Lyminster Church can be seen more clearly than before. The line of sight towards it follows a trackway which still runs from Lyminster towards the Arun and, on the other side of Lyminster, continues to the village of Poling and, beyond, Angmering, and it may be that the track leads from there to what was once a crossing of the Arun at this point.

As the outskirts of Arundel are approached the most prominent features of the town's skyline – the Castle, St. Nicholas's Church and the Cathedral – can be seen with increasing clarity, and the structure of the town is easier to understand than when one is walking round it.

On the further bank a mill building, once the South Marshes Windmill but now without sails and in private residential use, is to be seen. The route runs under the A27 and then through a comparatively new housing development, along to the right past River Terrace and into the old part of the town at Tarrant Street. No. 48 has a plaque to George MacDonald, author and poet, who lived in the house while Minister of the Arundel Independent Church, a building which is now an antiques mart.

When the King's Arms is reached, the route turns to the right down Arun Street, which has cottages in various materials including flint. At the end of Arun Street is a garden with lavender and other bushes, overlooking the river. The route continues alongside the river through a short footpath and then River Road (with an old shipyard building to the left) to the bottom of the High Street. The walker may well want to seek refreshment in Arundel at this point, and this seems a suitable point at which to sketch in an outline – it can be no more – of the history of the Earls of Arundel and Dukes of Norfolk, of the Castle and of Arundel itself, before suggesting an itinerary around the town.

CHAPTER 4.

The Earls of Arundel and Dukes of Norfolk

The Castle's domination of the Arundel skyline is an apt symbol of the rôle which it has played in the life of the town for almost a thousand years. In the relaxed, still slightly feudal, atmosphere of modern Arundel it is easy to imagine those who held the Castle, masters of all they surveyed, passing on from generation to generation a peaceful position of lordship over the town and its surroundings. In reality, however, the national position of the successive families concerned drew them for several centuries into turbulence and violence far from normally peaceful Arundel.

William the Conqueror assigned a part of Sussex with Arundel as its focus to Roger de Montgomery, a leading member of the Norman nobility who had been made Earl of Shrewsbury. Roger had not taken part in the Conquest, having been adviser in Normandy to William's wife, the Duchess Matilda, during William's absence in England.

The first upheaval came after William's death in 1087. He had left Normandy to his eldest son, Robert, and England to William Rufus, the second son. Roger de Montgomery, basing himself in Shrewsbury and in association with other Welsh border barons, joined in an unsuccessful rebellion in support of Robert's claim to the English throne. In this instance, backing the wrong side had no disastrous consequences, and Roger returned to royal favour. Roger arranged for the division of his lands after his death, his younger son Hugh taking the English possessions. Hugh, like his father, rebelled against William Rufus, and died fighting in Anglesey. His elder brother, Robert de Bellême, who already owned the family estates in Normandy, now took over the English ones also.

Robert de Bellême continued the family tradition of rebellion by taking up arms against Henry I in the interests of Robert Duke of Normandy. His castles, including Arundel, were taken, and he was banished to Normandy, where he conducted a reign of terror. Robert de Bellême's destabilising effect on Normandy was a factor in encouraging Henry I to invade it. All his property was confiscated to the Crown following the defeat of the Duke of Normandy's forces (and capture of the Duke himself) at the Battle of Tinchebrai in 1106; so ended the Montgomery connection with Arundel. Robert de Bellême died in captivity at Wareham in Dorset in 1118 and William succeeded to his father's inheritance in Normandy.

Henry I left Arundel to his widow, Queen Adeliza, who married William de Albini. The Albini family was of Breton origin and William's father had the title of chief butler to the King. William de Albini supported Matilda, Henry I's daughter and Adeliza's stepdaughter, against Stephen. Matilda arrived at Arundel in 1139 to assert her claim to the throne, and was besieged there by Stephen, who decided to let her escape to the west of England. William then changed his allegiance and supported Stephen, subsequently helping to bring about good relations between Stephen and Henry of Anjou, Matilda's son, who, when he became king as Henry II, rewarded William with the Earldom of Arundel.

It is now generally considered that the numbering of the Earls should start at this point, as the Montgomery Earls did not hold this specific title.

William's grandson, another William, was for a time closely associated with King John. He died returning from Crusade. There were two further Williams in the succession, the second of whom, the fifth Earl, died without issue in 1263.

This last William was succeeded at Arundel Castle by his nephew John Fitzalan who was not, however, styled Earl of Arundel. The Earldom was therefore in abeyance until about 1293 when Richard, John's grandson, is recorded as having the title of Earl. This lapse in the title has led some authorities to break the continuity of numbering of the Earls, calling Richard, like the William who founded the Albini line, the first Earl. I feel that this can confusing and I have maintained a single sequence of numbers, regarding Richard Fitzalan as the sixth Earl.

Richard took part in Edward I's wars. His son Edmund, seventh Earl, was caught up in the civil strife which characterised the reign of Edward II, and was beheaded at Hereford 1326, having fallen foul of Queen Isabella and her lover Roger Mortimore. Under an Act of Attainder (an Act of Parliament registering conviction for treason and declaring all property forfeit to the Crown) Arundel was granted to the Earl of Kent, but it was restored to Richard the eighth Earl, who served in Scottish wars, then won a naval victory over the French at the Battle of Sluys in 1340, subsequently fighting at Crécy in 1346 and at the siege of Calais, which took place in 1346 - 1347.

After Richard's death in 1376 his son, also called Richard, succeeded as ninth Earl. Reference is made in subsequent chapters to his noteworthy contribution to Arundel through the foundation of Maison Dieu and of Arundel College, in association with which he rebuilt the Parish Church of St. Nicholas. Nationally, he was active in both military and naval spheres, becoming Admiral of England. Unhappily, he fell victim to the political intrigues which beset the reign of Richard II and was executed for treason. This did not prevent him from being revered for his good works.

Richard's son Thomas restored the family fortunes by successfully plotting, along with his uncle the Archbishop of Canterbury, to replace Richard II with Henry Bolingbroke. After Richard's deposition, Archbishop Arundel crowned Henry in Westminster as Henry IV and Thomas was restored to his father's position at Arundel. After Henry IV died, Thomas went on to serve Henry V with distinction, in offices which included that of Lord High Treasurer. He died in 1415 of dysentery contracted at the siege of Harfleur.

Thomas was succeeded by his great-nephew John, a soldier, whose son the twelfth Earl, also called John, won military glory in the Hundred Years' War. He died in 1435 and was succeeded by his son Humphrey who died in childhood, with the title passing to his uncle William, who successfully navigated the stormy waters of the Wars of the Roses and died at the Castle in 1487.

William was succeeded by his son Thomas and grandson William, the latter a close friend of Henry VIII. William's son Henry, who succeeded in 1544 as the seventeenth Earl, was a suitor of Elizabeth I, but is described by J. E. Neale in his famous biography of the Queen as "rather silly and loutish". He was later associated, along with the Duke of Norfolk, in the Ridolfi plot to which further reference is made below. He avoided trouble sufficiently, however, to die at his London home Arundel House, in 1580.

It is at this point that the Dukedom of Norfolk comes into the story of Arundel. Henry's son of the same name died in 1556 at Brussels as a result of a fever caught while on an embassy to the King of Bohemia, and his daughter Mary becomes his heiress. She married, in the year of her brother Henry's death, Thomas the fourth (Howard) Duke of Norfolk, whose career is summarised below, but sadly died in the following year soon after giving birth to her son Philip, who in due course became the first Howard to hold the Earldom of Arundel. The Howard family, the origin of which can be traced back to East Winch near King's Lynn, was one of the greatest in England. It was set on its upward path in the thirteenth century by Sir William Howard, a lawyer who became Chief Justice of the Common Pleas. The family advanced through military distinction and favourable marriages, a notable step being the marriage in about 1420 of Sir Robert Howard to Lady Margaret Mowbray, elder daughter of Thomas Mowbray, Duke of Norfolk and Earl Marshal of England.

The lack of male heirs to the Mowbrays put the Howards into the line of succession to the Dukedom of Norfolk. Sir John Howard, Robert's son and a strong supporter of Richard III, received the Dukedom in 1483, and died at the Battle of Bosworth along with Richard III in 1485. His son Thomas also fought on the losing side at Bosworth, but he restored the family name and became a leading statesman and military figure of Henry VIII's reign, leading the English army to victory over the Scots at the Battle of Flodden in 1513.

The Howards inherited from the Mowbrays Kenninghall, said to have been one of the finest Tudor houses in England. Near the Norfolk/ Suffolk border, it was rebuilt by the third Duke as his principal seat but largely demolished in 1650.

Like Thomas Mowbray, Thomas Howard was appointed Earl Marshal, a post which in 1672 came to be an hereditary one held by the Dukes of Norfolk. The position is one of the great offices of State, having, among other responsibilities, an important role in the organisation of State ceremonies such as coronations. Deputy Earls Marshal – known as Knights Marshal – were often appointed, serving during the minority or infirmity of the Earl Marshal. Before an Act of Parliament in 1824, Protestant deputies were needed when the Earl Marshal was a Roman Catholic, as was usually the case. It was normal for these deputies to be members of the extended Howard family.

Thomas was succeeded by his son the third Duke, also called Thomas, two of whose nieces, Anne Boleyn and Katherine Howard, were married to Henry VIII and later executed. Thomas, having advanced them as part of his political plans, did nothing to save them. Eventually Thomas himself fell from favour with Henry VIII, partly through the behaviour of his brilliant but headstrong son the Earl of Surrey, who among his other accomplishments was a poet whose work has retained its appeal across the centuries. Surrey was executed on the flimsiest of charges; Thomas was saved because Henry VIII died just before his execution was due to take place.

The fourth Duke - another Thomas - succeeded his grandfather in 1554, and settled naturally into a leading role in the kingdom. Thomas was related to Elizabeth I, was the only Duke in the country, had great estates and also many accomplishments including interests in scholarship and architecture. Unhappily, the tragic fate which so often stalked the family struck Thomas in full measure.

It was the misfortunes of private life which paved the way to Thomas's political disaster. Three times Thomas became a widower, and it was his unmarried status which led to a plan in which his ambition overreached itself, to marry Mary Queen of Scots. Elizabeth was mistrustful, and Thomas became enmeshed in an intrigue known as the Ridolfi Plot. Ridolfi was a Florentine banker whose plans involved an invasion of England by the Duke of Alva, the Spanish Governor of the Netherlands, in support of a rising designed to put Mary Queen of Scots on the throne instead of Elizabeth. Perhaps one should say his purported plans, as it has been suggested that he was a double agent. Many circumstances of the plot remain obscure and the atmosphere of conspiracy and double-crosses would make a suitable theme for John le Carré. The outcome was the Duke's trial for treason, his attainder, and execution in 1572, with the confiscation of the family estates. These included Arundel Castle and the Fitzalan estates in Sussex, linked with those of the Howards as a result of Thomas's marriage, mentioned above to Lady Mary Fitzalan, the daughter of the twentieth Earl of Arundel. Although the Howard family was to show constant resilience right down to the present day, the downfall of the fourth Duke marked the end of an era; never again would the family fully return to its splendid – and dangerous – position at the heart of the nation's political affairs.

Thomas's son Philip is now perhaps the best remembered of all the Howards. He had inherited the Earldom of Arundel through his mother, and his father's disgrace did not initially affect his career at Elizabeth's court. His life took a new turn, however, on his conversion to Roman Catholicism - his father, unusually in the family, had been a Protestant. It is not easy, even now, to regard the religious controversies of that time in a dispassionate light. On the one hand, there is no question about the bravery and sincerity of the Roman Catholic priests and laymen who maintained their faith in the face of persecution. On the other hand, Pope Pius V had in his bull *Regnans in Excelsis*, issued in 1570, proclaimed Elizabeth's deposition and absolved Englishmen from their oath of allegiance to her. It is hardly surprising, therefore, that Elizabeth and her government regarded the Roman Catholic faith as a threat to what we would call national security.

It was in this atmosphere that Philip decided to flee the country. He was intercepted, arraigned before the Star Chamber, committed to the Tower, and after tension had been increased by the Spanish Armada, tried for treason. In spite of the deficiencies in evidence he was found guilty, condemned to death and returned to the Tower. Elizabeth did not sign the death warrant, but Philip was not told this, and his imprisonment in the Tower - grim in any circumstances - was made worse by the fact that he believed he might at any time face execution. In 1595, shortly before he died, he asked to see his wife and children, but Elizabeth would not allow him to do this unless he renounced his faith, which he refused to do. Philip was canonised by Pope Paul VI in 1970.

It is beyond the scope of this book to describe the general history of the members of the Howard family, such as Lord Howard of Effingham, who commanded the English fleet against the Armada; this narrative must confine itself to tracing briefly the story of the Earls of Arundel and Dukes of Norfolk. Phillip's only son Thomas was restored to the Earldom of Arundel by James I in 1604. Known as the "Collector Earl", Thomas was a patron of the arts and took a close interest in the history of the Howards. He had a somewhat chequered political career, but by the 1630s had achieved a position of dignity in the life of the nation which, if it did not fully match the status of some of his ancestors, was by no means unworthy of the family tradition. He was not, however, to be granted a tranquil old age, for he lived to know England engulfed in Civil War and Arundel Castle a centre of battle. At least he was not to see this happen with his own eyes, for his last years were spent in Italy.

Thomas's son Henry fought on the Royalist side in the Civil War, but generally did little to add distinction to the family's name. Henry's eldest son Thomas's mental balance was adversely affected by illness, but this did not prevent the Dukedom bring restored to him during the reign of Charles II. The next eldest son, another Henry, conducted the affairs of the Dukedom and eventually succeeded to it, but he was a victim of the religious tensions of the time and spent an increasing amount of his life at his house near Bruges.

Henry's son - another Henry - succeeded his father as the Seventh Duke. A pragmatic man, he did a great deal to consolidate the Howard position. Nevertheless, he did not exactly have a quiet life; with him, the often tragic character of the family history turned to farce; he initiated a divorce case, which was robustly defended by his wife, and the hearings before the House of Lords became something of a public entertainment.

Henry died in 1700, and was succeeded by his nephew Thomas, a person of strong religious views in the Catholic tradition usually - although as we have already seen not universally - adhered to by the Howards. Although he did not play a prominent rôle in politics, he was accused of involvement in a Jacobite plot and, like a number of his predecessors, was imprisoned in the Tower. Henry thereafter concentrated on looking after his estates, which included undertaking some work at Arundel Castle, although he visited the Castle rarely.

This concentration on family estates was continued by Thomas's son Edward, the ninth Duke, who succeeded in 1732. Edward's life was one of placid consolidation of the family position, in keeping with that calming of the more extreme political and religious passions which marked the course of the eighteenth century. On his death in 1777, the Dukedom passed to Charles, the grandson of a brother of Thomas and Henry, the fifth and sixth Dukes. Charles, a somewhat reclusive man, seems to have been rather overawed by his role as the tenth Duke, but his son, also called Charles, who succeeded him in 1786, was a hard-living, hard-drinking Whig, who used Arundel Castle for entertaining. His work on the Castle and the grounds is outlined in the following chapter. Charles's enjoyment of his traditional ducal rôle, and his radicalism, found expression in a dinner and entertainment he put on at Arundel in June 1815 to celebrate the six hundredth anniversary of the signing of the Magna Carta. It was all some way from the austere pieties of one strand in the Howard tradition; but the religious element in that tradition was far from exhausted.

Charles had no direct heir, and on his death later in 1815 the Dukedom passed to Bernard, great-grandson of another brother of the fifth and sixth Dukes. Bernard, the twelfth Duke, was a man of strong Roman Catholic views and a leading advocate of Catholic Emancipation which he saw as enabling members of his faith to make a full contribution to the mainstream of British life. He had the satisfaction of being able, under the terms of the 1829 Emancipation Act, to take his seat in the House of Lords.

Bernard's son Henry succeeded as thirteenth Duke in 1842, a man very conscious of the dignity of his position. In his time Queen Victoria and Prince Albert visited Arundel Castle, a successful social event. His chaplain Canon Tierney was the author of *The History and Antiquities of the Castle and Town of Arundel.*

Henry's son, of the same name, succeeded as fourteenth Duke. A very devout man, he was more influenced than his predecessors by the continental tradition of Roman Catholicism. He devoted much of his income to religious and charitable causes. He held the Dukedom for only four years, dying in 1860. His son - another Henry - lived until 1917, a tenure of the Dukedom which provides a sort of bridge from the historic past into a world we can to some extent recognise as similar to our own.

Nevertheless, the social and economic context of the Duke's life was very different from that which obtains today, and the Duke's cast of mind was also one scarcely familiar now. He carried on with his father's tradition of devoting substantial sums of money to good works, and he had a particular interest in the commissioning of buildings, both religious and secular, the evidence of which is inescapable in Arundel. He built a new Roman Catholic Church for Arundel, the Church of St. Philip Neri, now the Cathedral of Our Lady and St. Philip Howard. As will be seen in Chapter 7, the current appearance of the Castle owes much to him.

On the national scene, Henry as the leading Roman Catholic layman in the country had an active involvement in matters related to his faith, including relations with the Vatican. Among other examples of his public service he held the office of Postmaster General, and his interests extended to local government, not only in Sussex but in London where he was a member of the London County Council and the first Lord Mayor of Westminster.

Henry's son Bernard brings the Dukedom fully into the modern world. He maintained the family tradition of adaptation to the interests of the age; for if at one time our national preoccupation had been war, high politics, or religion, what could be more English in the second half of the twentieth century than devotion to cricket? In addition discharging the usual ceremonial duties of a Duke of Norfolk, including those of the hereditary position of Earl Marshal, Bernard was president of MCC and manager of the English cricket team on its tour of Australia and New Zealand in 1962-63.

Bernard died in 1975 and was succeeded by Miles, the seventeenth Duke, the great grandson of Edward, brother of the fourteenth Duke. Miles, a professional soldier, was succeeded in 2002 by his son Edward.

CHAPTER 5.

Arundel Castle and Priory

It is not the intention of this chapter to attempt to duplicate the detailed descriptions in the guide book on sale at the Castle but instead to provide historical background on the Castle, the Fitzalan Chapel and Arundel Priory especially as they have reflected the personalities and circumstances of Earls of Arundel and Dukes of Norfolk.

Although a Saxon origin has been claimed for the Castle, firm knowledge starts with Roger de Montgomery. The broad plan of the Castle derives from his time; the central fortified mound (motte) with upper and lower courtyards (baileys) protected by a curtain wall.

The only building which survives from Roger de Montgomery's time is the Gatehouse, which was subsequently protected by the Barbican, built by Richard Fitzalan, the ninth Earl, to whom reference has been made in the previous chapter, as part of his strengthening of defences of Castle and town which also included the building of the town wall. Of the Gatehouse itself only the lower part is as Roger de Montgomery left it, the upper part having been rebuilt by Richard. Between Roger de Montgomery and Richard, the major builder at the Castle was William de Albini, who was responsible for the stone keep on top of the motte, for work to the curtain wall and for the Bevis Tower which is to be seen to the left of the Keep as one approaches the Barbican. William's wish to strengthen the Castle was very understandable given the political instability of the time.

Formerly visitors to the Castle entered through the Barbican and Gatehouse but entrance is now through a gateway to the south, so there is less of a sense of the depth of medieval defences at the then Castle entrance.

During the thirteenth and fourteenth centuries the Castle developed towards the building which we now see, with its rôle as a home and centre of feudal life becoming more prominent. Of the work at that time the most spectacular feature was the great hall. This was in the approximate location of what is now the Barons' Hall, on the southwest side of the south bailey. By the end of the sixteenth century the residential quarters at the southeast corner of that bailey had been extended towards the hall to the west, closing off the south side of what was then a quadrangle.

Arundel Castle from the south: the towers on the left (west) are nineteenth century; in the centre is the dining room, incorporating the medieval chapel

A phase in the life of the Castle of which there is now little physical evidence - save for marks of cannonballs on the Barbican walls - is the Civil War siege of December 1643/January 1644 to which reference is made in the following chapter. In October 1649 the Council of State of the new Commonwealth ordered the demolition of the fortifications of the Castle – the interpretation of this appears to have been to limit damage to what was necessary to render the Castle indefensible. Only limited efforts were made to restore the Castle to good condition until about 1720, when Thomas, the sixth Duke, undertook substantial restoration with a view to establishing the Castle once again as the primary seat of his family.

The restoration went considerably further under Charles, the eleventh Duke, whose substantial rebuilding included a Barons' Hall and Chapel, predecessors of those we now see. It was for his benefit that Hiorne's Tower was built as an example of the style of restoration which might be used. Charles consolidated the general position of the Castle in 1803 by diverting the London Road at the top of the High Street in a more westerly direction and by erecting a wall on the north side of that road, protecting the privacy of the grounds. He also expanded the Castle land to the north, forming the Castle Park as it now exists.

It is, however, to Henry the fifteenth Duke that we owe the Castle in its present form. His building programme started in the late 1870s. The east wing was extended to the north, beyond the library, to provide a suite of private rooms, and the south and west wings were reconstructed. It is to this phase of the Castle's history that we owe the two cylindrical towers, one at the south-west corner and the other in the west front about half way to the Gatehouses. The work of rebuilding included the Barons' Hall and the Chapel, the work, as already mentioned, of Charles the eleventh Duke. The architect of the Chapel - as of much of Duke Henry's work – was Alban Buckler.

Whether Duke Henry was well advised to embark on such an extensive reconstruction of the work of Duke Charles is very much a matter of opinion. His accurate restoration of the surviving medieval elements of the Castle and of the Fitzalan Chapel is open to much less question.

The Early history of the Fitzalan Chapel is outlined below, in the context of Arundel Priory. The Chapel had been damaged and used as a stable by Parliamentary troops during the Civil War, and by the eighteenth century was in a very poor condition. The action authorised by Duke Charles to remedy this situation was most unfortunate. The partly-decayed roof timbers were cut through and allowed to fall into the Chapel, where they did a great deal of damage to stalls and tombs, and an anachronistic slate roof was installed.

Duke Henry's restoration was on more authentic lines, and gave us the Fitzalan Chapel as we now see it, with its remarkable collection of tombs of Earls of Arundel and Dukes of Norfolk prompting

Arundel Priory and the south-west corner of the Castle

thoughts both of transience and permanence. Were Philip Larkin, in his poem *An Arundel Tomb*, to have been writing about this place, he could have been said to have caught the atmosphere with remarkable accuracy and sympathy. He writes of the tomb of an Earl of Arundel and his wife whose effigies hold hands, the emotions of life communicated to us through the sculptor's art. In his words the effigies

Persisted, linked, through lengths and breadths
Of time. Snow fell, undated. Light
Each summer thronged the glass. A bright
Litter of birdcalls strewed the same
Bone-riddled ground...............

Perhaps a little disappointingly, however, the tomb concerned is located not in this Chapel but in Chichester Cathedral.

The Chapel was originally part of Arundel College, the other surviving elements of which constitute Arundel Priory, which can be seen to good advantage from the London Road. The College, founded in 1380 by Richard the twelfth Earl, replaced the Benedictine Priory of St. Nicholas endowed by Roger the first Earl, which had fallen on hard times. The Priory buildings were demolished as was the old Parish Church. The College was built around a quadrangle, on the north side of which was the Chapel, now the Fitzalan Chapel. Although the sharpness of the distinction between the Fitzalan Chapel and the Parish Church of which it appears to be a part derives, as explained in Chapter 7, from the Reformation, the function of the Chapel was always distinct from that of the Church, and part of the Chapel's role was, from the beginning, that of a memorial to the Fitzalan family. The Chapel was designed by William de Wynford, notable as master mason of New College Oxford and Winchester Cathedral.

In 1544 Arundel College was suppressed by Henry VIII and the buildings, except for the Chapel and the Master's Lodgings, were partly demolished and allowed to fall into ruin. Charles the eleventh Duke, other aspects of whose buildings have already been described in this chapter, put in hand the repair of what college buildings survived. As part of the restoration, an Oratory was provided: this is now the theatre mentioned in Chapter 7. The College buildings became a convent in the time of Henry the fourteenth Duke, and provided accommodation for a school and, after the buildings ceased to be used as a convent, a children's home; they now house a residential care home run by the New Order of Malta Homes Trust.

CHAPTER 6.

History of Arundel

Aspects of Arundel history have been brought out in the previous two chapters; further aspects will appear in the following one. It is the purpose of this chapter to provide a historical summary, concentrating mainly on the town rather than the Castle.

The first inhabitants of what we now call Arundel who have left us evidence of their presence are the Belgic people who are thought to have built what is known as the War Dyke (although the function of this earthwork is disputed) which runs from the Arun west of North Stoke to Whiteways Plantation west of the A284, as well as the rampart mentioned on the next page. A Belgic settlement in Arundel Park known as Shepherd's Garden has been excavated. The discovery of the remains of a Roman villa by the Arun, at the western end of Tarrant Street, provided evidence of the next phase of Arundel's existence.

Little is known of Saxon Arundel; a reference to the manor appears in the will of Alfred the Great and the Domesday Book tells us that in the time of Edward the Confessor there were, among other features, a port and an early version of the Church of St. Nicholas. The picture becomes much clearer, however, after the Norman Conquest. Roger de Montgomery not only built the Castle but also established Arundel as a Borough, with rights of self-government, in 1086.

The relationship between Castle and town has remained, naturally enough, a very close one from those early days until now. Adeliza, the wife of the fourth Earl, for example provided a new bridge across the Arun and an associated causeway across adjacent marshy land.

Richard, the ninth Earl, protected the town by building a wall, which ran west of the edge of the Castle moat near the Bevis Tower to St. Mary's Gate north-west of St. Nicholas's Church, then across the line now taken by the London Road and down what is now called Mount Pleasant (formerly Poorhouse Hill).

However pervasive the influence of the Castle, the town flourished in its own right, with its dignitaries led by the Mayor, its right to hold a market, and from 1295 until the Reform Bill of 1832 its sending two Members of Parliament to Westminster. Progress was by no means untroubled; in 1338 half of the town was destroyed in a fire and the Black Death struck ten years later. The town's concerns were in no way of such significance to the nation as the activities of the Earls of Arundel and Dukes of Norfolk, but Arundel was thrust rudely onto the national stage during the Civil War.

At the end of 1642, with the Civil War only a few months old, Sir William Waller, commander of the parliamentary forces south of the Thames, arrived at Arundel on his way to Chichester. The Castle was lightly held by Henry, son of Thomas the "Collector Earl"; Waller seized it with a force of 36 men, not one of whom was killed. The ease with which the Castle was taken possibly indicates support for the parliamentary side among the townspeople.

A year later, there was a change of fortune when Lord Hopton, whose advance across the Weald had been assisted by hard frost, took the town on behalf of the King; the odds against the parliamentary garrison of the Castle were so great that the Castle was surrendered. Within less than two weeks, however, Waller, helped by the same weather conditions which had previously aided Hopton, had returned to Arundel, and the royalist besiegers became the besieged. Sir Edward Ford, the commander of the royalist garrison, employed as a first line of defence the Belgic earth rampart and its extension described in Chapter 7, but this was soon forced and the royalists were confined to the Castle. Some of the residents of Arundel took refuge in St. Nicholas's Church; they surrendered when the Parliamentary forces threatened to burn them out. The parliamentarians subsequently used the tower of St. Nicholas's Church as a gun platform. The Castle sustained for seventeen days a siege which had its civilised moments - during a parley the defenders said that they desired "sack, tobacco, cards and dice". In order to stop the Castle's water supply, Swanbourne Lake was drained. The problems of defending the Castle were compounded by differences among the garrison's commanding officers. Following the failure of an attempt at relief by Hopton the situation of the garrison was clearly hopeless, and the royalists surrendered on 6 January 1644; some thousand prisoners were taken. Waller repaired defences before he left the town. In October 1649, after the end of the English Civil War, most of the Castle was demolished, as mentioned in Chapter 5. In 1659, ten years after the decision to demolish most of the Castle, demolition of the town wall was ordered.

The restoration of Charles II, and with him of the Church of England, in 1660 soon brought with it political changes to the town. Under the Corporation Act, as clarified by the Act of Conformity of 1662, the Mayor and Corporation were required to take communion according to the rites of the Church of England, which as Presbyterians they refused to do. They were replaced by a new, Anglican Mayor and Corporation.

After the upheavals of the seventeenth century, Arundel's concerns were once again mainly with local rather than national matters. In 1724 the wooden bridge over the Arun was replaced by a stone one, which lasted until the present bridge was built in 1935. In 1773 buildings were demolished to form the Market Square at the bottom of the High Street. In 1785, an Act of Parliament "For the better Paving, Cleansing and Lighting the Streets, Lanes, Ways and Passages within the Borough of Arundel, in the County of Sussex; and for removing and preventing Incroachments, Obstructions and Annoyances therein" marked a further stage in "tidying up" the town. Charles Howard, subsequently the eleventh Duke of Norfolk, and the Mayor and Burgesses of the town were appointed as Commissioners to administer the provisions of the Act, which included a ban on letting off fireworks in the street. The Act specified that the Commissioners should hold their first meeting at the Norfolk Arms, recently built with money advanced by the Duke, so they no doubt embarked on their duties with a degree of conviviality.
As is evident from its architecture, Arundel was substantially rebuilt in the eighteenth century, and in the early nineteenth it reached what was perhaps the height of its prosperity. The population rose

from 2,188 in 1811 to 2,803 in 1831. Trade increased because of the improved navigability of the Arun arising from the harbour improvements at Littlehampton in 1798, fine new houses were built, a theatre opened, and Arundel became socially fashionable. A new town hall - at the east end of Maltravers Street - was completed about 1836. However, the economic significance of Arundel was starting to diminish with slackening of trade, a tendency which continued in spite of the coming of the railway in 1863.

As the nineteenth century progressed, however, it saw a remarkable programme of works by the Dukes of Norfolk. The story of the Castle at that time has been given in Chapter 5; that of what was then the Church of St. Philip Neri is set out in Chapter 7; the rebuilt Castle and what is now the Cathedral of Our Lady and St. Philip Howard represent only the most prominent of Ducal initiatives, others including the laying out of Mill Road and the building of the mock-Tudor post office when the fifteenth Duke was Postmaster General. The benefits to the town were not only physical but also economic through the employment of local people on the works.

During the twentieth century, the pattern of economic activity in Arundel changed markedly, with a decline in manufacturing and in the disappearance of the once-important port, and a diminished role for agriculture; tourism has become increasingly important, and many residents now earn a living outside the town. Arundel continues to flourish, showing no evident signs of the adverse economic conditions obvious in other towns.

Path along Mill Road, Arundel

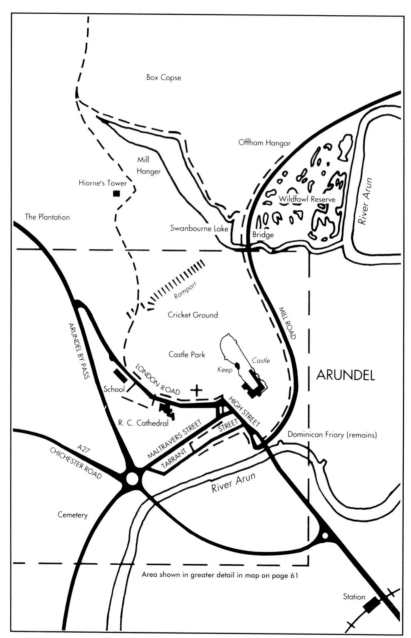

Arundel and its environs. Scale 1:17,500 - 3.5 inches to one mile.

CHAPTER 7.

Walk around Arundel

Distance: About three and a half miles.
Walking Conditions: Roads; paths, mostly firm, but includes the
                        climbing of a path which is slippery in wet
                        weather.
Station: Arundel.

From Arundel Station, where the route of this chapter starts, the pathway along the busy A27 is followed to the left past the Arundel Park Hotel with Arundel Castle prominently in view. The road is crossed at traffic lights, followed to the right, and crossed again to a pathway on the left. Arundel Bridge, which is soon reached, replaced in 1935, as mentioned in Chapter 6, a bridge which was built in 1724, itself the successor of previous bridges going back to Norman times.

The prominent building a little to the right as one crosses the bridge is the Post Office mentioned in Chapter 6. Beyond the bridge the route continues to the right along Mill Road. On the right are the remains of the south range of a thirteenth century Dominican Priory. Unfortunately it is not now possible to trace on the ground the full scale of the Priory but further remains can be seen behind a hedge on the other side of the road. Beyond the Priory is the new Arundel Museum and, on the left, the entrance to Arundel Castle. The Museum provides an excellent introduction to the history of Arundel and the surrounding area –the display is to be followed in an anti-clockwise direction. The history of the Earls of Arundel and Dukes of Norfolk is to be found within a circular display area. There is a great deal of interest to see in Arundel and this chapter cannot, for reasons of space, give anything approaching a comprehensive account. Readers may wish to supplement what follows with one of the leaflets available at the Museum.

The route continues along Mill Road which crosses a bridge at the outfall from Swanbourne Lake – there is an adjacent footbridge. From the footbridge can be seen the former Arundel Castle Dairy building which replaced the watermill which gave the road its name and which is thought to have been on the site of one recorded in the Domesday Book as having belonged to Earl Roger. Near the old Dairy building is Swanbourne Lodge, one of the Castle Lodges, now a tea house. Swanbourne Lake itself is used for boating; almost surrounded as it is by steeply rising ground, it presents an idyllic picture.

A short distance beyond Swanbourne Lake, on the right, is the Arundel Wetland Centre, with the steep Offham Hanger (a hanger being a wood on a hillside) rising to the left. The Centre is run by the Wildfowl and Wetlands Trust, whose first and best known reserve is that at Slimbridge in Gloucestershire, and aims to provide areas where the public can see a wide variety of waterfowl, both native species and those from far afield. The Centre consists of a complex of lakes and ponds with surrounding vegetation, with some areas designed to show habitats in various parts of the world. While it may lack the wide horizons of the Trust's better-known reserve of Slimbridge, it has an attractive setting and that and the variety of ducks and geese which are to be found make it well worth a visit.

From the Centre, the route returns to Swanbourne Lodge and Lake. Here it is of course possible to return to Arundel via Mill Road, but the recommended route takes the path on the north side of Swanbourne Lake past the Lodge and a refreshment kiosk. It is possible to walk along the south of the lake, but the path is muddy after rain – the northern path is firmer, although parts require care.

At the far end of the lake a gate with the sign, "Livestock. Keep dogs on lead", is reached. To the left is the path which follows the southern side of Swanbourne Lake. The recommended route crosses the stile by the gate and, following the yellow arrow, takes the path which leads to the village of Houghton. In due course the path is crossed by another, the junction being marked by a Public Footpath sign. The path to the left is taken; it climbs gently, with a bank of trees to the right. Where the trees end, giving way to grass on both sides of the path, there is a fine view to the left. A gate is then reached, with a

A Lane in Arundel

Cathedral of Our Lady and St. Philip Howard

59

yellow arrow pointing right. This direction is followed up a slope. Another yellow arrow is then followed, keeping Hiorne Tower on the right. This Tower was built in 1790 by Francis Hiorne for the eleventh Duke.

A roadway is reached which is followed to the left. It curves to the right and shortly an earth rampart, regarded as the work of the Belgic people who built the War Dyke to the north, may be discerned to the left. The road passes Park Lodge and the entrance to the cricket ground on which the opening march of each overseas team's tour used to be played against the Duchess of Norfolk's XI. The further section of rampart visible on the left is not thought to be contemporaneous with the rest, but may date from 1643, when the Royalists were defending Arundel. The route continues to the main (London) Road, turns left and passes St. Philip's Roman Catholic Primary School and the Roman Catholic Cemetery. The St. Mary's Gate Inn on the right is a reminder of the existence of the Mary Gate, where the London Road used to pass through the town walls. The Gate, the first conclusive reference to which was in 1343, had a Chapel as its top floor – the Chapel of Blessed Mary Over the Gate. This Chapel was destroyed during the Civil War, and when Charles, the eleventh Duke of Norfolk, diverted the London Road, the Mary Gate, situated north-west of St. Nicholas' Church, was incorporated into the Castle grounds. The eleventh Duke restored a top floor to the Gate, which remains now as he rebuilt it.

The route now reaches the Roman Catholic Cathedral of Our Lady and St Philip Howard, built as the Church of St. Philip Neri under the patronage of Henry the fifteenth Duke in 1870-73. The architect was Joseph Hansom, the founder of the Builder magazine and inventor of the Hansom cab. George Myers was the builder. Hansom's original designs showed greater elaboration than the building we now see, which reflects the Duke's own views. There was an intention to have a spire over the north-west porch but the foundations were not thought strong enough to carry it. When the Roman Catholic Diocese of Arundel and Brighton was established in 1965 the Church became a Cathedral, its name including a commemoration of St. Philip Howard.

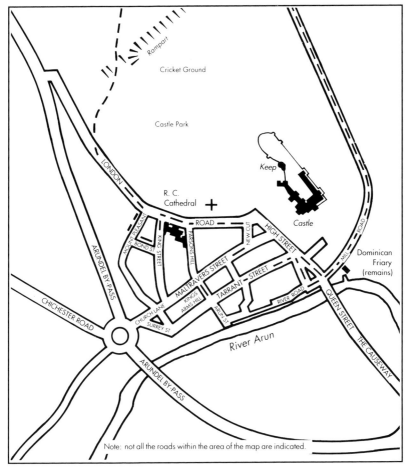

Arundel and its environs. Scale 1:17,500 - 3.5 inches to one mile.

On the opposite side of London Road, a little further on is St. Nicholas's Church. The history of this Church is closely involved with that of Arundel Castle and Priory, and that relationship is brought out in Chapter 5.

There was originally a Saxon Church of St. Nicholas on this site, which was recorded in the Domesday Book. After the Conquest, this Church appears to have been subject to enlargement or rebuilding, and the resulting Norman Church was itself demolished, and the current building erected, by Richard the twelfth Earl in association with his foundation of Arundel College. The design of that part of the building which is now the Parish Church was the responsibility of Henry Yevele, the master mason whose best known work is the naves of Canterbury Cathedral and Westminster Abbey.

After the suppression of Arundel College in 1544 the chancel of the Church, which was also the Chapel of the College, was sold along with the rest of the College by Henry VIII to Henry the twentieth Earl of Arundel, for £1,000. The subsequent history of the Chapel is outlined in Chapter 5; as a private Roman Catholic Chapel, it now had a different denominational identity from the Anglican Parish Church. The iron grille which already separated the Church from its Chapel now had more profound symbolic significance; the grille remained locked for centuries, the keys in the possession of the Earls of Arundel/Dukes of Norfolk.

During the nineteenth century, restoration of the Church was undertaken by Sir Gilbert Scott, and in 1976 work took place to bring its layout more in line with current thinking. In 1977 the iron grille was opened and the Church used for a single service for the first time since the Reformation.

At the north-west corner of the churchyard are sections of wall which incorporate stonework which has now been identified as the remains of the Maison Dieu. This was founded by Richard, the fourteenth Earl of Arundel, in 1395 as a hospital/almshouse. Like Arundel College which was mentioned in Chapter 5, the Maison Dieu was built round a quadrangle. It consisted principally of a chapel, refectory and living accommodation. The establishment was run by a "Master", a priest who combined administrative and spiritual roles. The inmates, who wore a brown woollen garment, were expected to be scrupulous in their religious observances and to engage in useful work, unless prevented by infirmity. The Maison Dieu was dissolved in 1546.

Beyond the Church is Arundel Priory, the history of which is outlined in Chapter 5. The former Oratory – the first part of the building one reaches on passing the Church – is now a theatre, the remainder a residential care home run by the Order of Malta Homes Trust.

The route continues along London Road a short way, and then turns to the right down New Cut (just before the High Street and opposite the road sign to Dorking and London) to Maltravers Street. Across that street to the left is the somewhat forbidding early nineteenth century Town Hall.

Maltravers Street, which is now followed to the right, is, however, predominantly eighteenth century, the buildings showing sufficient variation to relieve what can sometimes be the monotony of the Georgian style. At No. 16 there is a plaque indicating that it was the residence of Dr. G. W. Eustace the local historian, who was author of *Arundel: Borough and Castle*.

The route continues west along Maltravers Street to its junction with Parsons Hill (running north) and Kings Arms Hill (running south). From this junction there is a good view up to the Roman Catholic Cathedral. The route follows Kings Arms Hill down to Tarrant Street.

Tarrant Street is altogether livelier than Maltravers, with shops - antique shops being a speciality – and restaurants. Among notable buildings is the Nineveh Chapel. The name, with its obscure biblical reference, derives from an earlier secular building on the site. The current building, dating from 1838, was constructed as a Congregational Chapel and now houses an antique market. The route follows this street to the left, towards the High Street.

Its position rising uphill from the bridge gives the High Street a certain natural excitement; in climbing it, one is rewarded with views across the Downs. The two sides of the Street differ in the character of their buildings. On the east, eighteenth-century brick buildings predominate, the Norfolk Arms, a former coaching inn, providing the focus. To the west, there is much more variety of style, and roofline, with what was once the West Sussex Gazette building, a notable example of the mock-Tudor style which is such a feature of the nineteenth century phase of Arundel's development.

Once the High Street has been explored, the route continues over the bridge at the bottom of the hill and along the Arun to Burpham and beyond.

The River north of Arundel

CHAPTER 8.

Arundel to Amberley

Distance: About six miles.
Walking Conditions: Mostly paths, some of which are muddy in wet wether; short distances on roads with little traffic.
Station: Arundel, Amberley.

At the far (southern) end of Arundel Bridge a path to the left which has a signpost indicating that it is part of the Monarch's Way is taken. This Way is part of a national network of long-distance paths established in the interests of walkers. It is based on the route thought to have been taken by Charles II during his escape following defeat at the Battle of Worcester in 1651 – a journey during which he is said to have hidden from his Parliamentary pursuers in an oak tree. The route goes past a private garden, then continues to the left to reach the river by a narrow path to the side of a fence surrounding the Fitzalan Swimming Pool. It follows the river past jetties with moored boats, with Arundel Castle always dominating the skyline. As the path approaches the railway, and by a sign giving the River Arun speed limit as 5 knots, it crosses a stream, controlled by a sluicegate, which winds away to flow beneath the A27 Arundel-Worthing road west of the station, and rejoins the Arun at Tortington. Ahead is the line of the Downs; on the right is the wooded high ground of Warningcamp. With a bit of luck, there will be some swans on the river; all-in-all an idyllic scene.

Walkers can follow the river round its next loop, but the recommended route goes across the railway. Caution should be taken when crossing the line, indicated on the notice. Just past The Gatehouse a path indicated by a footpath sign leads off to the left of the road. The path is protected by trees and shrubs, a welcome

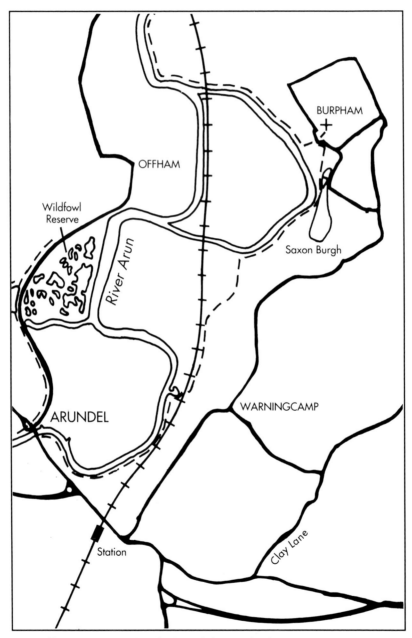

Route map, section 3: Arundel to Amberley station, part A.
Scale 1:25,000 - 2.5 inches to one mile.

source of shade on a hot day. The route continues, nearly parallel with the railway on the left, until it bears right through a gate, and then turns to the left, as indicated by a signpost. The route continues with a barbed wire fence to the right and a curved line of trees to the left. It then crosses a stile on the left and continues through a field, with the direction marked by a footpath sign. It goes across a stream and then after some sixty yards turns to the left, over a stile.

The route is as indicated by the middle arm of the Public Footpath sign, straight across the field in front. Shortly it reaches a combined ditch and hedge which is kept to the right.

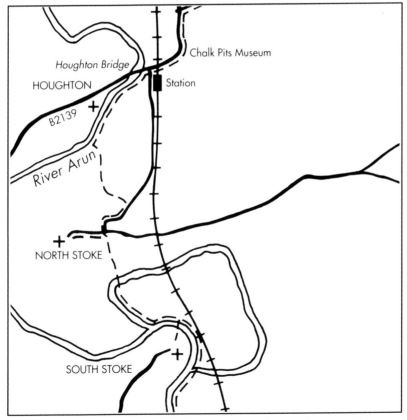

Route map, section 4: Arundel to Amberley station, part B.
Scale 1:25,000 - 2.5 inches to one mile.

The route, running through a gateway to the right, brings one back to the river. Here it has an aspect very different from that at Arundel, for this is not the main channel, which was diverted to the west of the railway on the construction of the line to avoid the cost of two swing bridges, but the original channel, heavily overgrown by reeds and other water-loving plants. The route continues to the right along the river.

There is a stile by an Environmental Agency notice and the route goes over this and the bridge beyond. Having passed another stile one encounters steeply rising ground ahead. A further stile has to be negotiated and the recommended route follows the steep path ahead which has steps cut into it. Where the path emerges from the trees there is a large open space protected by a fence, which is followed to the left. Although the fact may not be immediately obvious, the route is now running round Burpham Camp, a large earthwork which may originally have been an Iron Age promontory fort, and was certainly used by the Anglo-Saxons, being one of the "burghs" which were vital strong points in the defensive system established by Alfred the Great and his son Edward to provide protection from the Danes. The responsibility for the repair of these "burghs" and for their defence in time of war rested with the local population - a sort of early version of the Home Guard.

The route continues towards a large pavilion behind which can be seen the steeply rising north bank of the Camp, a rampart to defend the vulnerable end which was unprotected by rising ground. The route runs through a gap in this bank. On the right is the George at Burpham, the village pub. The cottage opposite, close against the embankment and now much altered, was home in the early years of the twentieth century to John Cowper Powys, the lecturer and writer. His novels, *Wolf Solent, A Glastonbury Romance*, and *Weymouth Sands* are not very familiar to the modern reader. One may surmise that he was not enthusiastic about the more rumbustious side of village life, particularly, perhaps, as represented by the clientele of the then George and Dragon, for he tells us in his *Autobiography* how he used to sneak out of his little enclosed garden and make his way furtively among the graves of the churchyard to reach the Downs without having to speak to anyone.

St. Mary's Church, Burpham

Beyond The George is a road junction - the road ahead climbs and soon reaches St. Mary's Church. This early Norman (perhaps Saxon) Church was substantially rebuilt in the twelfth and thirteenth centuries, with additions in the nineteenth century in a happily compatible style. Mervyn Peake is buried in the churchyard alongside his parents. As a novelist Peake is now much better remembered than Powys, thanks at least in part to the adaptation for television of his *Gormenghast*, set in a fantastic castle. The lively - some might say hyperactive - imagination needed to conceive such a bizarre world may have had its roots in China, where Peake was born in 1911 and spent his formative years. He lived for a time in a thatched cottage in Wepham, a hamlet just south of Burpham.

From the Church, the route returns downhill and turns to the right at the junction following, again downhill, a small road marked by a "No Through Road" traffic sign. The route follows along a path with a fence to the right and then continues to the right towards

The gravestone of Mervyn and Mary Peake,
St. Mary's Church, Burpham

the river, initially through overhanging trees and then, by way of a small barred gate, through a field. A lane leads in from the right, providing access for farm vehicles, and their tracks can be seen leading to a gate into a closely-cropped field. These tracks are not followed - at this point the route turns left and then crosses the railway line. Particular care is needed here. Shortly past the railway line one reaches the point where the old course of the river joins the new cut. From this point the atmosphere becomes more remote and indeed lonely. Along these stretches of the river it is not difficult to imagine more turbulent times when the surrounding downs, now so domesticated, could have contained hidden menace. Such oppressive thoughts are, however, dispelled when the little hamlet of South Stoke appears on the opposite bank. Shortly before the hamlet is reached, there is marshy ground to the right of the path, and this is the point at which yet another diversion of the river took place, for this marshy tract marks the old course of the Arun and the current course represents a cut made in 1839 to bring the river closer to South Stoke and improve navigation.

A footbridge takes one over the river into South Stoke. The route follows a track bearing a little to the right which brings one to a road; a path leads to the left to St. Leonard's Church. The Church is essentially the original eleventh century building, with thirteenth century lancet windows. The nineteenth century brought "restoration" and a curious, to my mind somewhat Alpine, spire. Once when I was there sheep were grazing in the churchyard, an economical way of keeping the grass under control. The hamlet of South Stoke consists mainly of cottages, but has two buildings of substantial size whose Georgian frontages conceal an earlier origin; the Old Rectory (behind the east end of the Church) is fifteenth century, and South Stoke Farmhouse, overlooking the river, is sixteenth.

The Arun valley from above South Stoke

The route involves retracing one's steps over the bridge and turning left along a signposted path which initially follows the embankment. Shortly the footpath bears right, opposite South Stoke Farmhouse on the other side of the river, and runs through a wood, keeping on its left the old course of the river; this is the upstream end of the disused loop of which the downstream end was crossed before South Stoke was reached. The path crosses this residual stream by means of a suspension bridge. There is no footpath sign at this point, but the route goes straight up a slight hill towards buildings on the brow, which are part of North Stoke. It crosses a farm track, goes over a stile and on reaching a lane the route turns left, passes a telephone box, and follows through to the Church.

Like its Southern cousin, North Stoke is a hamlet which has the river on three sides, and is cut off from through traffic. While the churches of this part of Sussex are often notable for their evocation of the past, that at North Stoke is exceptional in the extent to which it retains a medieval atmosphere. Built between the Norman period and the fourteenth century, it has some fine stone carving of foliage and an animal's head, floral patterns can still be seen on the walls, and the east window and south transept east window contain panels of what is said to be the oldest stained glass in Sussex, Next to the Church is Manor Farm, in Georgian style. From this point the route returns to the telephone box and then turns left along Stoke Road.

The route follows Stoke Road downhill. As the road levels out a path is singposted to the left. It is possible to continue along the road, but the recommended route runs along this path which follows what was the bank of the river before the "Houghton cut" was made at some point before 1724 - the course of the rest of that original loop of the river can be detected to the west of Stoke Road. The path is somewhat overgrown at first but when it reaches the river it provides pleasant views of Houghton on the opposite bank. The route continues to the right until a small bridge appears on the left. This bridge is crossed and the route turns to the right on the path which leads up to Houghton Bridge. Caution is needed at this point because the bridge has no footway and vehicles customarily cross it quite fast - drivers will not be expecting the sudden appearance of a pedestrian in the roadway. The route now runs to the right.

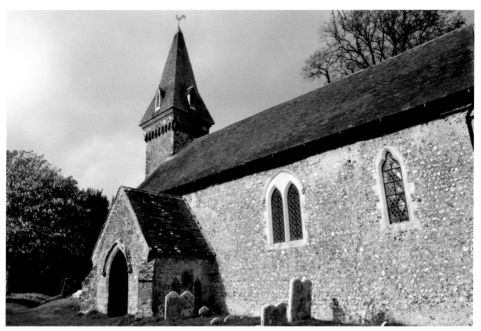

St. Leonard's Church, South Stoke

St. Mary's Church, North Stoke

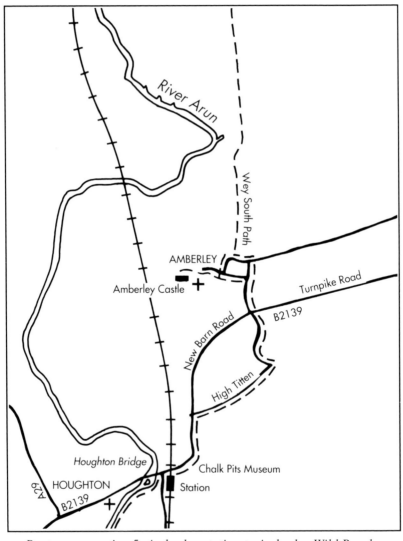

Route map, section 5: Amberley station to Amberley Wild Brooks.
Scale 1:25,000 - 2.5 inches to one mile.

CHAPTER 9.

Amberley - Chalk Pits Museum, Castle and Village

Distance:	About two miles.
Walking Conditions:	Mostly roads; a short stretch of path which is muddy in wet weather. It should however be noted that this walk leads on to those in Chapters 10 and 11, with no station until Pulborough. Before attempting these walks as a sequence, account should be taking of the overall distance, and of the comments about walking conditions in Chapter 10.
Station:	Amberley.

This chapter picks up the route at the east end of Houghton Bridge, the point reached at the conclusion of the preceding one, but the walker can reach the same point quickly from Amberley station. As the route away from the bridge is followed the old toll house is to be seen on the left, prominently marked as The Turnpike – named after the eighteenth-century Turnpike Acts which led to major improvements in the country's road system.

To the right is to be seen the chalk face of the hillside, not a natural cliff but the result of excavation by generations of workmen. The chalk was converted, by burning, into lime, the main use of which is as a constituent of mortar and cement, although it also serves as a fertilizer. The technique of burning chalk in kilns to make lime was known to the Romans, and there is reference in the will of the Bishop of Chichester dated 1382 to the right to dig and burn chalk at Amberley.

There is no continuous record of the chalk pits between the medieval period and the end of the eighteenth century. Early in the nineteenth

The Turnpike and chalk face

century there were several separate producers working the pits. The commercial development of the site was assisted by improved access through work to increase the navigability of the lower Arun and the building of the Wey and Arun Canal, and in 1863 by the coming of the railway – in 1870 a spur line gave direct access to the pits. In 1876 John Pepper, who was originally a shipowner but later a farmer and brickmaker, had along with his son Thomas taken over the business of one of the established firms at the Amberley pits, and by the end of the century their firm was in possession of the whole site.

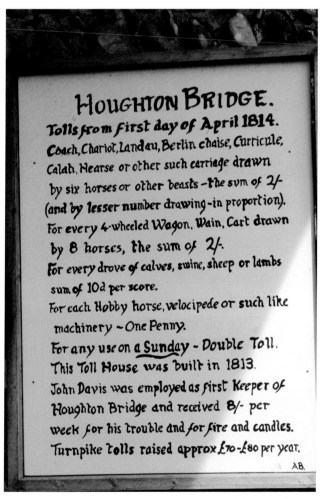

The Turnpike - notice of tolls for Houghton Bridge

The works closed in the 1960s and have been converted into the Chalk Pits Museum, which is to the right under the railway bridge opposite the station. The site is so large that bus and train services are provided for visitors. While restoring and showing what might be termed the industrial archeology of the site such as the kilns is, of course, a key objective, the Museum has expanded far beyond that core purpose. There are many exhibits unrelated to the original works on the site, such as the replica of a 1920s Southdown Bus Garage with a collection of vintage buses. The Museum also features workshops in which traditional crafts are carried out. It is rightly an important tourist attraction although the purist might feel that visitors should be given greater assistance in distinguishing which buildings are part of the original works.

On leaving the Museum the route crosses the main B2139 road and turns to the right along the footpath. After a while the path is separated from the road by a hedge. Shortly after the end of the hedge the route turns up a minor road, High Titton. A path running to the right, with vehicle access barred by two wooden posts, leads to an open space which gives a "bird's eye view" of the Chalk Pits Museum. High Titton meets a lane, which is followed down the hill. Towards the bottom of the hill branches meet overhead, creating an enclosed, private world. At the end of the lane the road joins the B2139. The route crosses the road (care is needed) following the signs to Amberley Village Stores and Amberley Village Tea Rooms.

Amberley is one of the oldest settlement sites in the valley, and is first mentioned in 683. It was a centre for agricultural activity, with many of the buildings in the village having originally been used for farm purposes, and some still in such use. Its exceptional attractions have attracted artists, and it is now understandably a magnet for tourists.

One approaches Amberley passing the village's Church of England school on one's right. To the left of the lane there is a small stream, leading appropriately enough to Stream Cottage, said to have been built in 1587. Then one reaches the modest intersection known as the Square with, on the right, another sixteenth century building, Old Stack Cottage. Here the route turns left, along Church Street, a road bordered by houses of exceptional aesthetic and historical interest. On the north side is Old Postings, once the Post Office but originally built - although never used - as a butcher's shop. On the south of Church Street the buildings start with Forge Cottage, occupied by the village blacksmith till 1955; then there is the Old Brew House, which provided a service to the Vine House next door when that building was a beer house, known as the Golden Cross in the nineteenth century. Next is the Malt House, originally used, not surprisingly, as a store house for malt.

On the north side of the road, the cottages include The Old Bakehouse, the name indicating its former rôle in the life of the village, and the studio which belonged to Gerald Burn, a painter and etcher. Back on the south side there is Drewitt's farm, a partly flint farmhouse, followed by a public footpath to the Recreation Ground opposite North Way. After that comes Boxwood, once the home of Fred Stratton, another member of the village's artistic colony, and then The Haven, which was once a butcher's shop. The Chapel a little further on opened in 1867; it is now Amberley Village Pottery. Next door is the curious Manse, which has an oriental flavour. The route continues along the south side of Church Street, past a reed-thatched barn. Next to the barn is Oak Tree House. The House is formed from three former cottages; the one at the east end used to house the Clarkson Room, where one of the first Dame Schools in Amberley was established in the middle of the nineteenth century.

Beyond Oak Tree House is the Vicarage, situated behind the Church Hall. The Vicarage was completely rebuilt in the first half of the eighteenth century, although Elizabethan cellars remain. The Church Hall was built in 1964, replacing two successive earlier buildings on the site.

It is thought that there was a Saxon Church at Amberley, but no trace of it remains. St. Michael's Church was originally built under the direction of Bishop Luffa, the founder of Chichester Cathedral. The nave and roof survive from that building. It was expanded in the latter half of the twelfth century, the large north and west windows dating from that time. The long chancel, with its lancet windows typical of Sussex churches, is thirteenth century, from which the tower is also thought to date. Although the Church is not without impressive qualities, it does not to my mind have the same atmosphere as some of the others in the area.

Amberley: The Alley, looking south towards the Manse

Amberley High Street

Past the Church, a path runs under the formidable curtain wall of Amberley Castle and the route follows this. The wall, with the gatehouse, was built about 1380 when defensive measures were considered necessary against the French and also, it seems possible, against the local peasantry! It protected an earlier manor house, probably twelfth century, which is now at the south-east corner of the complex. The west side of this building - facing into the courtyard - is most attractive.

The Castle has had a varied history. It was founded, like the Church, by Bishop Luffa, and it was Bishop Rede who fortified it, and also built the Great Hall. This building - much of which has been demolished - lies on a north-south alignment behind the kitchen which is the easterly, and most substantial, projection from the north wall, and was originally attached to the manor house. It appears that the last Bishop of Chichester to live at the Castle was Robert Sherburne (1508-1536); in 1538 the Castle was let to Sir William Shelley and Sir William Goring. During the Civil War John Goring held it for the Royalists, and it has been claimed that the Castle was sacked by Parliamentary forces, although there appears to be no evidence for this.

The lease changed hands frequently after that time, by sale as well as by succession, until the Castle was sold outright in 1872 to Lord Zouche of Parham, and then purchased by the Duke of Norfolk in 1893.

In 1925 Thomas Emmet, an artist of independent means, became the owner. His wife Evelyn - his widow in 1934 - had a distinguished career in public service which included membership (representing North Hackney) of the London County Council and then of the West Sussex County Council. She became in 1955 MP for East Grinstead and in 1964 was given a life peerage as Baroness Emmet of Amberley. Her service to the Conservative Party included chairing the Party's Annual Conference in 1955. She died in 1980. The Castle is now a hotel.

From the end of the Castle wall one returns along the path and then continues along the north (left) side of Church Street, past Amberley House, built in 1911 by an American. The lane leading to the left, known as The Alley (formerly Smock Alley) is worth exploring.

Naillards, on the right of the Alley as one walks up, is called after a family of that name. After The Alley, the route continues along the north side of Church Street to North Way (formerly known more picturesquely as Hog Lane), which is then followed. On the left as one turns up North Way is Old Place, formed from the combination of three or four cottages. Stott's Cottage, opposite, is named after the artist Edward Stott who lived there.

As North Way turns to the right, a path leads off to the left; this is the next direction the recommended route will take. Before following that path, however, it is worth exploring Amberley a little further. On the right of North Way is the thatched North Road Farmhouse. Beyond that, running downhill from the Black Horse, is the delightfully-named High Street, with little in common with the many suburban roads known by that name. On the left hand side is the village shop.

Retracing one's steps one comes back to the already-mentioned path from North Way leading into Amberley Wild Brooks, one of those wetlands which are a diminishing feature of our landscape.

Amberley Castle and St Michael's Church

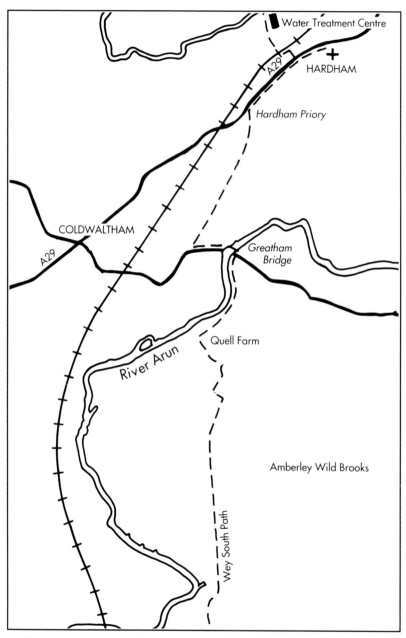

Route map, section 6: Amberley Wild Brooks to Hardham Church.
Scale 1:25,000 - 2.5 inches to one mile.

CHAPTER 10.

Amberley to Hardham Church

Distance:	About three and a half miles.
Walking Conditions:	Paths, mostly quite firm, but one section marshy as explained below; a stretch of busy road.
Station:	None.

The route runs straight on into the Brooks. The area is one of rough grassland and drainage ditches, sometimes flooded in winter, and supports a considerable variety of wildlife. Drainage of the area has been proposed, but a public enquiry in 1978 rejected the idea: a notable success for the conservationists. It should be said that the path through the northern part of the Brooks is muddy even in dry weather, and can be very difficult during periods of heavy rains. Stout footwear is always desirable on this route, and in the winter walking through the marshy area may well be impracticable, and it would be advisable then to pick up at a later stage the route suggested in this chapter.

The path on the original route is initially firm and chalky, but in due course it comes to consist of an earth embankment raised above the level of the surrounding fields.

Some distance ahead, what appears to be the main pathway turns left. The route continues ahead as indicated by a Public Footpath sign and past a board giving information about Amberley Wildbrooks. Although the direction is clear, the path is no longer raised and care is needed on the marshy ground.

There is a stretch of woodland on the left and then the route goes across two small wooden bridges taking the route across drainage channels. There is a post with a black on yellow footpath sign pointing ahead and then a field is reached and is crossed, keeping a fence on the left. At the top corner the route goes to the left following the Wey South Path sign and then turns to the right through a gate opening with a latch on the right. Where the path meets another at a T-junction the route turns left and then right by the entrance to Quell Farm House. The route runs through a farmyard and continues to follow the path until it divides. The left fork is taken over a cattle grid. As the Arun comes into view a grassy path marked by a rather ambiguous Public Footpath sign leads off to the left to follow the river along to Greatham Bridge.

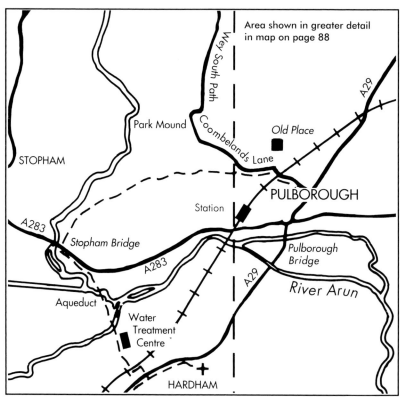

Route map, section 7: Hardham Church to Pulborough.
Scale 1:25,000 - 2.5 inches to one mile.

This bridge was built between 1307 and 1327 by Sir Henry Tregoz, the Lord of the Manor of Greatham. The western half has been little altered since that date; the eastern half has been cut away, and the piers now carry iron girders, with an unfortunate effect on the overall appearance of the bridge.

The course of the river under Greatham Bridge marks yet another of the human interventions in the Arun's course. Originally the river flowed (on a line indicated by the current parish boundary between Parham and Coldwaltham) along a meander which ended just below Greatham Bridge, remaining south of the Greatham - Coldwaltham road until it crossed it at the point where the road now intersects with the disused canal described later. The river then followed a course north-west almost to the village of Coldwaltham, where it turned to the north-east at the far side where the railway line now runs. It then looped below the higher ground on which Hardham Priory stands to turn south, joining the current course of the river less than half a mile north of Greatham Bridge. This lost meander of the Arun was known as the Widney, and the meadows between it and the current main stream of the river remained known as "The Widneys". There is no certain information about when the present route of the river under Greatham Bridge was cut, but it seems reasonable to suppose that it was at the same time as the bridge was built.

Greatham Bridge is crossed, and a short walk along the road brings one to a concrete and tubular steel fence on the right (now mainly obscured by brambles) which marks where the road crosses the route of the disused canal. This canal was built in 1785 and ran from a point almost a mile south of Greatham Bridge up to Hardham Mill on the River Rother close to its junction with the Arun, to save three miles on the Arun route through Pulborough. In spite of the advantage given by the shortening of the route, it is quite surprising that anyone should have embarked on the construction of this stretch of canal given the substantial obstacle of a ridge which had to be overcome. A quarter-mile long tunnel was dug under the ridge. J. B. Dashwood, in his *The Thames to the Solent* (1868), an amusing account of a boating trip from the Thames at Weybridge to the South Coast via the Wey and Arun Canal, describes going through this tunnel. He punted the boat

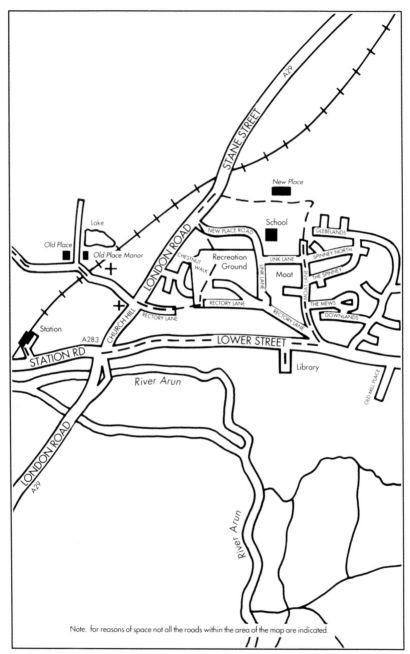

Town map of Pulborough. Scale 1:15,840 - 4 inches to one mile.

along by means of a boat-hook against the roof, which was covered with stalactites, and it took about ten minutes to reach the far end.

There is a stile towards the end of the fence (to the right of the road) mentioned in the previous paragraph with a Public Footpath sign and this path, which follows the path of the old canal, is taken. The path is rather overgrown although not difficult to walk. The route passes the boarded-up end of the canal tunnel, and after a short climb crosses a stile into a field, from which Hardham Priory is visible on the right. This Priory was founded by Sir William Dawtrey in the reign of Henry II. It was a small establishment, seeming never to have had more than six inmates. The Priors seem to have been unduly subject to the distractions of the world, including the opposite sex. One was deposed and another sent to Tortington Priory to reflect on the errors of his ways. In 1524, the then Prior admitted that he had stolen deer from the Earl of Arundel. The Priory was dissolved and sold in 1534. The Priory buildings are now part of a farm complex and are private property without access to the public.

At the top left hand corner of the field there is a gate which is crossed to give access to the A29. The route follows this road to the right, towards Pulborough. A walk of about half a mile brings one to the hamlet of Hardham, which is set along a winding street a little back from the main road. The Church is probably Saxon, for it is dedicated to St. Botolph, the Saxon patron of ports and river crossings (appropriate as the Church is so near Pulborough Bridge), and has the traditional Saxon square East End. The small windows high in the nave and chancel are also Saxon in character – the other windows are later, and the bell-turret and porch are Victorian. Roman tiles and bricks were used in the building of the Church - these probably came from the nearby Roman site.

In the south wall of the Church there is a squint, now blocked, which once gave a view of the altar and is the only surviving indication of an anchorite's cell which was built against the wall. The Church has fine early twelfth century wall paintings but unfortunately there is normally no access to them as the Church, like that at Climping, is kept locked for reasons of security.

St Botolph's Church, Hardham

CHAPTER 11.

Hardham Church to Pulborough

Distance: About four and a quarter miles.
Walking Conditions: Paths, mostly firm; stretches of road, some busy.
Station: Pulborough.

From Hardham it is possible to continue north along the busy A29 into Pulborough but the recommended route involves returning along it to a point, near where the path met it in the previous chapter, at which a road runs off to the right. The A29 is crossed to that road which is followed to a bridge over the railway line. At the end of the bridge there are two metal barred gates, with latches to the left. The route crosses a field to a similar gate and turns left and then right, following Public Footpath signs. A roadway is reached which follows the line of the old Pulborough to Petersfield railway, this section of which - going as far as Petworth – was opened in 1859. Some parts of the Pulborough to Petersfield line, which closed to passenger traffic in 1965 and to goods traffic in 1966, are open to walkers.

The route comes quite close to what was the junction of this branch line with the main line and then, following signs, turns to the left along a path. It has briefly followed not only the line of a former railway but also that of Stane Street, the Roman road from Chichester to London. There is nothing now to be found of this section of the road, but its line is followed by the A29 north of Pulborough.

The route leads past the Southern Water Services Treatment Centre to the River Rother, which is crossed by a bridge. The river (not to be confused with the East Sussex one of the same name) joins the Arun a little way to the right at the end of its course, which begins near Selborne in Hampshire, runs south to Petersfield and then to the east below the northern edge of the Downs before reaching this final, and it must be said not very attractive, stage of its journey.

The route - unsigned at this point - goes across a rusty metal barred gate to a modern bridge across the Arun, with a Public Footpath sign and metal barred gates at each end. The route takes one over the bridge and then to the left along the Arun, an idyllic scene at this spot. To the left is the entrance to the canal cut, built in 1794, which linked the Rivers Rother and Arun as part of the Rother Navigation to Petworth and Midhurst. The route then turns right to a stile next to a rusty barred gate. This leads to what was once the A283, but is now a minor road following construction of the new Stopham Bridge. This road is followed to the White Hart.

Stopham Bridge

This attractive public house stands at the east end of Stopham Bridge, good views of which may be obtained from the garden. Originally there was a ford at this site; it was replaced by a ferry, known as the Estover Ferry. The first bridge dated from the mid fourteenth century, and was probably of wood. In 1423 it was rebuilt in stone, and it remains unchanged to this day, with the exception of the centre arch, which was raised in 1822 to provide additional headroom for sailing craft. Stopham Bridge is a fine piece of architecture, much enhanced by its delightful setting. On the west bank of the river, party hidden by trees, is Stopham House. There have been houses at this site at least since Tudor times, but the present house is as remodelled in 1865 by Sir Walter Barttelot, whose ancestor John Barttelot acquired the Manor by marriage in the fifteenth century.

Stopham Bridge is now for use by pedestrians only, as a by-pass and new bridge conveying the A283 north of the old one were completed in June 1986. Some may feel that the proximity of the new bridge detracts from the beauty of the setting of the old one; on the other hand, the protection of Stopham Bridge from the rigours of modern traffic was obviously a very desirable step from the point of view of the preservation of its structure.

There is a bus service along the A283, and walkers wishing to break the route at this point can take the bus into Pulborough; the bus can also of course be used to rejoin the route if a walker has taken the A29 northwards option at Hardham. There is a Garden Centre at which refreshments are available on the north side of the A283, a short distance from Stopham Bridge going towards Pulborough.

From Stopham Bridge, the route crosses the A283 near the new bridge to where a Public Bridleway sign with a blue arrow points to a path, rising and curving to the right, which is followed. The route runs through woodland with, early on, a steep downward slope to the left. A sign is reached indicating that the Public Bridleway continues and that a Public Footpath, marked with a yellow arrow, leads to the right. The route continues straight ahead – the footpath goes down to the Garden Centre already mentioned.

After a while the route skirts the edge of the woodland area; to the right, across the fields, are fine views of the Downs; the tower of

Pulborough Church can be seen ahead. Traffic noise from the road
below only slightly disturbs the peaceful scene. The route passes a
fine stretch of pines to the left. A post with a blue arrow indicates
the path to be followed. The route continues beside a fence backed
by gorse bushes and then through a wood. Bearing right, it goes
by the side of a five-barred wooden gate, down a grey gravel path,
and reaches a lane. Across the lane is a post – the yellow arrow
is followed, taking the path. In the next field is a well-preserved
Second World War defensive position, once occupied no doubt in
much the same spirit as that in which the Anglo-Saxons looked to the
defence of the fort at Burpham.

The route follows downhill, giving a fine panorama of the Downs to
the right, until it reaches Coombelands Lane. It then turns right along
the Lane. On the left, down a path marked Public Footpath, are Old
Place and Old Place Manor, attractive fifteenth century buildings.
Old Place, the first to be reached, was originally a barn. With its
mullioned windows, well-kept garden, and lake behind, it has an
idyllic air. Once when I was there I saw a heron which was perched
on a pontoon in the middle of the lake, so still that for a moment I
wondered whether it was a sculpture, until it took off in majestic
flight. Old Place Manor is best viewed from the far end of the lake.
While interesting, it lacks the idiosyncratic, evocative quality of Old
Place.

Old Place Manor dates from the reign of Henry VI (1422-61) and
was built by Nicholas Apsley, although it has been subjected to
substantial alteration. Old Place (also altered) may well date from
the same time. The name of Apsley is now remembered because of
Apsley House in London, which was built (1771-78) by the architect
Robert Adam for Baron Apsley (subsequently Earl Bathurst), who
was descended from Nicolas Apsley. Apsley House was bought by
the Duke of Wellington's elder brother, and subsequently by the
Duke himself, as whose home it became famous as No 1 London.
Apsley House now faces the swirling traffic of Hyde Park Corner:
there could be no greater contrast to the peaceful surroundings of
Old Place.

The road is followed over the railway. A walker wishing to leave the
route at this point can take the footpath which follows the railway

Old Place

Old Place Manor from the lake

down to Pulborough Station. A little further on is St Mary's Church, which one approaches through the fourteenth century lychgate. The Church was originally Norman, but only the font survives from that time. The chancel is thought to be late twelfth or thirteenth century, while the nave, aisles and tower date from 1420-1430, and are in characteristic Perpendicular style. There is an oak screen by Sir Ninian Comper at the west end of the nave.

Past the Church, the route crosses the busy London Road into Rectory Lane, past the Chequers Hotel on the left. The lane passes the fine Old Rectory, built by the Rev. Francis Mose, Rector from 1720-1729. Past the Old Rectory is a dovecote originally in the Rectory garden. A little further on is the Glebe Barn. The route continues along the footpath and turns left at a Pubic Footpath sign, past the bowling green to the Recreation Ground, crossing it towards a housing estate, the cricket nets and hockey pitch being kept on the right and the cricket square on the left. As one approaches the houses, one discovers to the left what is described on a notice as a "Pocket Park" running along a stream. This park represents a commendable initiative, providing a pleasant stroll, with a fine display of daffodils in spring. The path through the park bridges the stream and leads on to New Place Road and then to London Road.

A few paces to the right along the London Road bring one to a minor road running to the right past signs saying "New Place Nurseries Quality Plants" and "Public Bridleway". This path is followed past allotments on the right.

A high wall on the left protects the former Manor House of New Place. In about 1450 this building, as part of the manor, came into the hands of Nicholas Apsley, already mentioned in connection with Old Place Manor. New Place as it now stands (and it is not open to the public) is predominantly sixteenth century. There is a gateway through which Elizabeth I is said to have passed when visiting the Apsley family in 1591 - that gateway is thought to have formed the entrance to a quadrangle, three sides of which were occupied by the mansion. Among the features of New Place is a curious chimney with a mullioned window at its base. In 1732, John Apsley sold the building to Henry Shelley of Lewes, who was related to the Horsham Shelleys who produced the poet. On the death of John Apsley, Old

Place Manor passed to Francis Mose of Petworth, thereby ending the Apsley connection with Pulborough.

The route runs along a path to the right of plastic greenhouses following the sign Public Bridleway. Past the greenhouses the path meets another at right angles to it; the route turns right at the junction, and follows the tree-lined path past a new housing development (Glebelands) on the left and St. Mary's Church of England School on the right. The path continues to the junction with Link Lane to the right and Spinney North to the left. The route continues straight ahead into Moat Lane. On the right is an open space across which a raised area with a moat around it can be seen.

The route continues along Moat Lane which runs into Rectory Lane, which is followed to the left into Lower Street. The route turns right at this point. It passes, or of course might divert into, the Oddfellows Arms, named after a charitable organization founded in the eighteenth century, and continues along Lower Street.

After a while houses no longer line the road, for Pulborough has developed as quite a dispersed town. The tower of St. Mary's Church appears on the high ground to the right. This rural scene offers only a short interlude, however, from the modern world, for there is heavy traffic at the mini-roundabout where Lower Street joins Church Hill, the A29. There are two attractive timber-framed cottages across the mini-roundabout, Skye Cottage and Horncroft, but for the pedestrian, crossing the road safely has to be the first call on attention.

The A29 crosses the Arun over a modern bridge, built in 1936. The earlier bridge, built in 1738 to replace a wooden one, remains alongside and is open to pedestrians. There was originally another eighteenth century bridge in Pulborough, Clement Bridge, which was close to the railway bridge, but this was demolished in the 1930s.

The route does not go over the bridge but continues along Station Road (A283) to Pulborough Station, where this series of walks ends. It has encompassed a wide variety of scene, built-up and rural, and has provided much opportunity for reflection on the complex natural and historical forces which lie behind what presents itself to our eyes. The past was not one long idyll, rudely interrupted by the modern world; it contained much violence, poverty and disease, as well as those happier features, such as a strong sense of community, which we now so often miss. I hope that this book has helped, to however small a degree, appreciation of the area it describes, and perhaps even of wider aspects of our inheritance.

Oddfellows Arms, Pulborough

FURTHER READING

A.H.Allcroft, *Waters of Arun*, Methuen, 1930.

J.R.Armstrong, *A History of Sussex*, Phillimore, 1961.

Peter Brandon, *Sussex*, Robert Hale, 2006.

D. Robert Elleray, *Littlehampton: A Pictorial History*, Phillimore, 1991.

Mark Turnham Elvins, *Arundel Priory*, Phillimore, 1981.

Robert H. Goodsall, *The Arun and Western Rother*, Constable, 1962.

Ian Nairn and Nikolaus Pevsner, *Sussex*, Penguin Books, 1965.

Joseph H. Preston, *Arundel: A History of the Town and the Castle*, Associated University Presses, 1993.

John Martin Robinson, *Arundel Castle*, Phillimore, 1994.

John Martin Robinson, *The Dukes of Norfolk: A Quincentennial History*, Oxford University Press, 1982.

Ivy Linda Strudwick, *Pulborough: A Pictorial History*, Phillimore, 1983.

H.J.F.Thompson, *Littlehampton Long Ago*, Printed by J.P. Ltd., Bognor Regis, 1974.

Reference has been made in Chapter 3 to the Sussex part of the Victoria History of the Counties of England, and the recent volumes in particular give a very detailed and scholarly account of the history of the area.

A History of the County of Sussex Volume V Part 1, ed. T.P.Hudson, Oxford University Press, 1997, covers Arundel, Climping, Ford, and South Stoke.

Volume V Part 2, Boydell and Brewer, 2009, covers Burpham, Littlehampton and North Stoke.

References to Amberley, Hardham and Pulborough are dispersed as these parishes are covered in earlier volumes which are structured in terms of subjects such as churches, roads, etc. rather than parishes.

BIOGRAPHICAL NOTE

John Adamson is an Oxford history graduate, a fellow of the Royal Geographical Society and a former local government officer. He wrote the first version of this book twenty years ago when his knowledge of, and affection for, the Arun Valley were already of long standing, and he has been able to bring further information and insights to the writing of this new edition.

A member of a number of organisations concerned with the conservation of buildings and the natural environment, John sees not only preservation but also renewal as important in town and countryside.

John co-edited (with Len Hudson) London Town Miscellany and went on to edit St George and the Chinese Dragon, an account by Lt. Colonel Henry Vaughan of the relief of the Peking Legations in 1900. His most recent book is Staines Preparatory School – Past and Present. He has also written magazine articles on aspects of the history of London and Buckinghamshire.